T0083436

IT'S ALL GOOD (UNLESS IT'S NOT)

The **ON CAMPUS** imprint of UBC Press features publications designed
for the diverse members of the university community – students, faculty,
instructors, and administrators. **ON CAMPUS** offers a range of interesting,
sometimes unconventional, but always useful information. All **ON CAMPUS**
works are assessed by experts in the field prior to publication. To ensure
ON CAMPUS materials are easily obtainable, they are made available
for free download in digital format or for purchase in print.

Resources for students are designed to help them successfully meet
the intellectual and social challenges encountered at university or college
today. The inaugural book in the **ON CAMPUS** imprint was the highly
successful *How to Succeed at University (and Get a Great Job!): Mastering
the Critical Skills You Need for School, Work, and Life*, which is also
available in French from University of Ottawa Press.

To find out more about **ON CAMPUS** books visit *www.ubcpress.ca*
or follow us on social media.

NICOLE MALETTE

IT'S ALL GOOD

(UNLESS IT'S NOT)

MENTAL HEALTH TIPS AND SELF-CARE
STRATEGIES FOR YOUR UNDERGRAD YEARS

UBC PRESS

This book is dedicated to my students
—N.M.

29 28 27 26 25 24 23 22 21 20 5 4 3 2

Printed in Canada on FSC-certified ancient-forest-free paper
(100% post-consumer recycled) that is processed chlorine- and acid-free.

Library and Archives Canada Cataloguing-in-Publication Data

Title: It's all good (unless it's not) : mental health tips and self-care strategies
for your undergrad years / Nicole Malette.
Names: Malette, Nicole, author.
Description: Includes bibliographical references and index.
Identifiers: Canadiana (print) 20200265970 | Canadiana (ebook) 20200266519
ISBN 9780774839013 (softcover) | ISBN 9780774839020 (PDF)
ISBN 9780774839037 (EPUB) | ISBN 9780774839044 (Kindle)
Subjects: LCSH: Undergraduates – Mental health.
LCSH: College students – Mental health.
Classification: LCC RC451.4.S7 M35 2020 | DDC 378.1/9713—dc23

Canadä

UBC Press gratefully acknowledges the financial support for our
publishing program from the Government of Canada (through the Canada Book Fund)
and the British Columbia Arts Council.

Printed and bound in Canada by Friesens
Set in Egyptienne, Goudy Sans, and Black Ground by Gerilee McBride
Substantive and copy editor: Lesley Erickson
Indexer: Patricia Buchanan
Cover designer: Gerilee McBride

UBC Press
The University of British Columbia
2029 West Mall
Vancouver, BC V6T 1Z2
www.ubcpress.ca

CONTENTS

KNOWING YOU'RE NOT ALONE

I thought university was going to be great. How could it not be? Television shows and movies made it look like it would be the most amazing time of my life. I'd get to meet new people, go to parties, learn new things, and develop skills to contribute to society in a meaningful way. I felt prepared for the transition: I had done well in high school, was involved in different sports and clubs, liked music, enjoyed travelling, and was interested in learning. I had even visited friends who had gone away to university and had stayed with them in their dorm rooms over holiday breaks. When I went away to school, I was convinced I was going to have a great time – just like them.

But I didn't.

Seeing college or university life on television and through my friends' experiences didn't prepare me for how hard it could be. My classes were huge, the lectures were sometimes difficult to understand, and they were full of people who seemed to have no problem following along. By Thanksgiving, my grades had fallen by at least 15 percent in all of my classes, and I had no idea why. I felt I was working just as hard, if not harder, than ever before.

Meeting people wasn't much easier. I chose to go to a different university from most of my hometown friends. I thought that because I was doing something different I'd have a more exciting social experience. But in reality all of the people I had known and relied on before university were no longer around. I tried going to Frosh Week events and talking to people in my classes, but no one seemed to have the same interests or experiences as me. Growing up in the country, I was used to being outdoors. I liked spending my spare time cycling, running, or going on hikes. Most of the people I met were from the city, had never been hiking, and had no interest in outdoor activities.

Frustrated with my deteriorating grades and lack of meaningful relationships on campus, I stopped leaving my dorm room. I started sleeping longer, exercising less, and eating more. Instead of doing my assignments, I used up all the hours in the day watching television. Sleep became the only reprieve from how terrible I felt. After a few months, even this stopped being enough, and I started having thoughts of ending my life. I worried that the university would kick me out if they found out how stupid and unprepared I was. I also thought that my family would be upset with me because they had given me every chance to succeed, and I was squandering the opportunity.

The feelings and beliefs that I developed about myself in my first year of university negatively impacted my school work, friendships, and romantic relationships throughout my undergraduate and graduate school experiences. Thankfully, conversations with friends and family members helped me understand that the way I was feeling wasn't okay and that I needed to get help. In second year, I started to talk to others, and I began to look online for strategies to deal with stress and depressive feelings. At this point, I was no longer in crisis, but my feelings were still having a negative impact on my friendships, my schoolwork, and family life. Even though I was talking to others, fear of what others would think of me for seeking professional help stopped me from accessing those resources. Four years later, I finally visited the on-campus counselling centre and started to participate in counselling services.

I found visiting the counselling centre a lot easier and more helpful than I had anticipated, and I continued to visit it throughout my master's and doctoral studies. I learned that I have both anxiety and depressive disorders, and after talking with caring counselling staff, I realized that mental illnesses are not uncommon among university students and that there are many strategies for dealing with them. I also learned that the negative feelings we have about ourselves and others with mental illnesses simply make things worse.

When I sat down to write this book, all the negative feelings that I had had about myself during undergrad came rushing back. I thought, *You're too dumb to write this book. No one will listen to you. The publisher made a mistake. It won't get published, and it will all be a giant waste of your time and theirs.* But then I realized that those feelings are part of why I'm writing this book and why I do the research I do. At the time of writing, I was completing my PhD, specializing in how institutional contexts influence university students' mental health and mental health service use. I also teach undergraduate courses and have helped connect numerous students to on-campus help services. Almost all of my professional life is now dedicated to trying to make things better for students, and this book is no different.

My personal experience and my work with students have taught me that most students don't ask for help. Most, like me, think they can fix their problems on their own, regardless of whether these problems are academic, social, financial, or emotional. But the reality is that only minor problems can be managed this way. I learned the hard way that taking advantage of the opportunities of a university education can at times depend on asking for help and developing mental health literacy.

The Importance of Mental Health Literacy

Mental health literacy is a term that came about after health professionals coined the phrase *health literacy*. People with health literacy have the skills needed to gain access to, understand, and use information in ways that promote and maintain their health. The term reflects an understanding that although individuals are their own agents, maintaining good health is a social process. We can sometimes figure out how to be healthy on our own, but we can't always get there by ourselves. The process involves working with others, using resources when needed, and sparking conversations to help people become more aware of what it takes to maintain good health.

By extension, mental health literacy has four elements:

- eliminating barriers to learning about mental health

- decreasing stigma related to mental disorders

- understanding how to obtain and maintain positive mental health

- understanding mental disorders and their treatments.

This book will enhance your mental health literacy on all fronts.

One of the main barriers to learning about mental health is the term itself. People often use *mental health* and *mental illness* interchangeably, as if they mean the same thing. The American Psychological Association defines mental illnesses as "health conditions involving changes in emotion, thinking or behaviour (or a combination of these things)." Mental illnesses are conditions that cause distress or problems for individuals in family, social, work, or school settings. In a given year, one in five adults will experience some kind of mental illness, most of which are treatable. By contrast, *mental health* refers to mental well-being – our emotions, social connections, thoughts and feelings, understanding of the world around us, and ability to solve problems and overcome difficulties. Everyone has mental health, just as everyone has health.

As you enter your undergrad years, it's important to understand that over the course of a lifetime not all people will experience a mental illness but that everyone will have experiences that challenge their mental health (just like we all experience challenges to our physical health but are not necessarily ill). Our experiences of mental health are not binary – we don't simply have good or bad mental health at a given time. There are different degrees of mental health that range on a continuum from a healthy mental state, to a reactive mental state, to an injured mental state, to mental illness. This book will enhance your mental health literacy by exploring these distinctions in detail.

It goes without saying that stress is a big part of the academic experience, and it can challenge your mental health. But it can also be positive. Stress generally occurs when we face situations that seem more demanding than we think we can handle. Sometimes those feelings can be useful. People can channel feelings of stress to focus their attention or fuel their work. For example, it's common to feel stress before a sporting event, a musical performance, or an oral presentation. Athletes and musicians learn to use stress to focus, push themselves, and adapt new techniques. And students can too. But it's important to understand that stress can also make people feel threatened or overwhelmed. Understanding how stress works and that it can be managed is a key tool for maintaining good mental health.

Another barrier to understanding mental health is the stigma attached to mental illness. Stigma is the negative ideas and misconceptions people have about those with mental illnesses. For instance, people might characterize those with depression as being lazy, stupid, or selfish or as untrustworthy, unreliable, or unemployable. This kind of thinking is socially constructed, meaning that these ideas are not real on their own but are made real by the way people think and talk about them. Stigma becomes socially acceptable when people start to think that those with mental illnesses are different from the general population. Then, as people discriminate against those with mental illnesses, they become victims who are systematically denied essential human characteristics. Individuals with mental illnesses and disorders often fear the consequences of disclosing their problems to others because they're afraid of what others will think of them. Stigma erodes their self-esteem, limits their social networks, and hampers their ability to succeed in school or in the job market.

Despite the negative opinions people might have about people with mental illnesses, few people who experience them are at risk to themselves or others. In fact, contrary to stereotypes, many highly intelligent, hard-working, and creative people have mental illnesses. An article in *Intelligence* published in 2018 indicated that more than a quarter of the members of Mensa, the high-IQ organization, had been formally diagnosed with a mental illness. Former Apple CEO Steve Jobs spoke openly about his struggle with depression, and Michelle Obama has discussed her struggles with panic attacks. In Canada alone, Olympic gold medallist Clara Hughes, actor Ryan Reynolds, comedian Jim Kerry, former NHL hockey player Theo Fleury, retired senator and military general Roméo Dallaire, and Margaret Trudeau (Prime Minister Justin Trudeau's mother) have all spoken out.

Stigma is particularly problematic in university settings because undergraduates are likely to experience stress and events and feelings that challenge their mental health but are unlikely to seek help to deal with them. Studies by Daniel Eisenberg and others show that undergrads rarely seek treatment. This can negatively impact their grades and chances of graduating. It also means that many people don't have the knowledge and insight to recognize when they need help. I hope that when you finish reading this book you'll have this knowledge, along with the power to change negative narratives about mental illness.

Throughout this book, I talk about different ways you can help others overcome stigma and what groups are doing to limit its effects. Understanding is the first step toward dismantling stigma. It involves recognizing our common humanity and bridging the perception that there is a divide between those who experience mental illness and those who don't. We all experience challenges to our mental health. How we treat others should reflect how we all want to be treated in our moments of need. We're all in this together.

In This Book You'll Find ...

In this book I draw on current research, my own experiences, and the experiences of other students to enhance your mental health literacy. Your time on campus might be different than mine, and your experiences might not exactly reflect everything written in these pages, but it's my greatest hope that you'll find some of it helpful for navigating your undergrad years, from making the transition to university and maintaining a healthy mind while you're there to knowing where and when to seek help.

The first two chapters are for new students, but I encourage everyone to read them because they include advice on things you might still be struggling with, and they might make you more aware of what other students are going through or have to offer. Chapter 1 opens with a discussion of the exciting opportunities and experiences that most students face when they make the transition to university, including living in dorm, having a roommate, and looking after your own finances. It includes advice for reducing your negative stress load to make the transition as smooth as possible. Part of creating the best university experience possible for everyone is fostering a campus atmosphere that values and supports diversity. Chapter 2 looks at the positive contributions and special challenges of first-generation, Indigenous, racialized, international, and LGBT2SQIA+ students.

Before launching into a discussion of the various strategies and techniques you can adopt to maintain your grades, enjoy an exciting social life, and preserve good mental health, Chapter 3 digs deeper into the distinctions between positive and negative stress and mental health and mental illness. Armed with these definitions, you'll be better able to assess the state of your own mental health as you engage in all areas of school life, from your studies (Chapter 4), to making time for friends and extracurriculars (Chapter 5), to enjoying campus party culture and staying safe (Chapter 6), to taking care of your mind and body through diet, exercise, and outdoor activities (Chapter 7). Chapter 8 will help you detect the warning signs of mental illness in yourself and others, and it describes what you can expect if you seek professional help.

Throughout the book, you'll find **Quick Tips** and **Quick Facts**, **Student Stories**, **Self-Care Strategies**, **FYIs**, and **Getting Help** features that will help you make the transition to university and achieve both personal and academic success while you're there. Reducing the stigma attached to mental illness has two components – speaking out and learning you're not alone. The tips, facts, and FYIs are self-explanatory. The **Student Stories** show you how other students have experienced challenges to their mental health. These are students who, like me, had certain ideas about what school would be like and found that reality didn't quite meet their expectations. They discuss solutions that worked for them. Maybe these strategies will work for you, maybe they won't. They're included here to illustrate that there are different ways of overcoming challenges.

As someone who struggles with anxiety and depression, maintaining a lifestyle that involves practising **Self-Care Strategies** has been extremely helpful for me, and studies have shown that adopting them is one of the best ways to maintain good mental health. When I start feeling stressed and overwhelmed, I know that I need to get away from my desk, go for a run, talk to someone about my problems, and think about what's best for my body in terms of food and rest. Although these things often get overlooked by students, they're some of the most important strategies for keeping your body and mind ready to take on the opportunities that university brings.

A big part of having good mental health literacy is also knowing what help is available and when to seek it. There are a range of mental health resources available to students across Canada, and the **Getting Help** features throughout this book will help you find them. Like me, you might experience ups and downs in college or university that you never anticipated, and you might experience challenges to your mental health at some point in your life. But you don't have to struggle through it alone. If there is one takeaway message I hope you get from this book, it's that there are people in your life and on campus who care about you and are ready to help (even if you don't know who they are yet). I want you to realize this and to feel empowered to reach out to others.

MAKING THE TRANSITION TO UNIVERSITY

The first day of kindergarten was pretty much the same for all of us. Adults bundled us up, snapped pictures, and sent us off to face a new world filled with strangers who would become our teachers, classmates, and friends. Even though we repeated this same routine every year, for many of us it never stopped being a nerve-racking experience. Who knew if you would get a good teacher or if your friends would be in the same classroom?

Starting college or university is no different. You get to see what it looks like on television and in the movies, but you don't actually know what your own experience will be like until you get there. If you live in residence, will you get a good roommate? Will you like your professors? Will your exams be really difficult? Will you make new friends? Even if you have friends and older siblings who have already gone to school and can answer some of these questions for you, university life is often a trial by fire.

This whole process can be daunting because students are expected to adjust to university life almost immediately. After taking part in a few Welcome Week activities, everyone – from parents, friends, and instructors to students themselves – might think everything is now "all good." Unfortunately, the idea of a quick-and-easy transition is a myth. Most students won't walk onto campus, attend a few orientation sessions, and then prosper throughout their undergrad years. There will be many rewards but also setbacks and disappointments. Going away to school is a process, one that takes multiple years and a lot of adjustment.

Quick Tip

Instead of thinking that you'll adapt to university as soon as you set foot on campus, try to think about your undergraduate years as part of a life process.

It's strange that we don't think of college life in the same way we think of our elementary and secondary school years. There are scores of books about how children develop and how our school experiences form us into who we are today. As a society, we expect kids to take years to learn new life skills, overcome personal challenges, and build important relationships with others. Unfortunately, we don't think about post-secondary education in the same way.

Instead of thinking you'll adapt to university life as soon as you set foot on campus, try to think about your undergraduate years as part of a larger life process – something that takes time, patience, and understanding to successfully navigate. This chapter explores some of the most common social, economic, and academic opportunities, challenges, and adjustments that students experience when they first go to college or university, and I'll give some suggestions for how best to handle them. Keep in mind that not every change will apply to you, but it's a good idea to read about other students' experiences to realize that you're not alone.

Moving Away from Home and Sharing Space with Others

Although some university students continue to live with their parents or guardians, many new students move away from home and into dormitories or off-campus housing. These students often find themselves in a new environment where no one is watching what they do or how they act. They leave family members (a source of protection and emotional support while they lived at home) behind and find them replaced with an institution and strangers. Unfortunately, universities and colleges aren't designed to nurture students in the same way that loved ones can and do, and realizing this can be hard. It can lead to loneliness, particularly when the routines and habits of family are gone and new routines and support networks on campus have yet to be found. Finding replacements for support networks takes time, and you might need to lean on pre-existing ones until you get better acquainted with campus life.

SELF-CARE STRATEGY
Maintaining Emotional Support Networks

Depending on your relationships with people back home, keeping up with old friends and family can be a great way to maintain emotional support while you face new experiences on campus. However, balancing new and existing friendships can be emotionally challenging and can take time away from settling into campus life.

If you still live at home or close to home, one way that you can manage these relationships is by setting aside time to hang out with both your on- and off-campus friends throughout the semester. There might be times when your social networks back home cross over into your on-campus social life, but most of the time, setting distinct times to hang out with each group will help you manage your social time in conjunction with your studies. To do this, try scheduling time with your on-campus friends during breaks between classes or at the end of the day. Having dinner with them, meeting for coffee between classes, or going out in the evening might be the most effective use of your social time with friends in that space. If you tend to go home on weekends, make that the time you get together with off-campus friends.

Balancing time between these two groups is a great strategy for keeping up emotional supports as you make the transition to university. However, make sure that you're not spending all of your time socializing with your off-campus friends and family (online or offline). Putting more time into social connections on campus can help you feel more immersed in campus life. Think about the relationships that are most important to you and what you want out of your campus experience, and then think about the ways that you can balance these relationships. Being at university is an opportunity for you to try things you've always wanted to try, to think about what you value in your relationships, and to make new friendships based on shared values (not just being in the same neighbourhood or high school).

Another thing to consider is that going away to school can be a good way to "start fresh." Maybe you have friends or family members that aren't emotionally supportive (or were even emotionally harmful). This is a good time to take a break from them and think about what qualities you want in your social groups.

Student Story...

My undergrad was a journey with a lot of ups and downs. I was proud of what I was doing at school – contributing to a body of knowledge – but there were many social forces that made it much harder for me to stay positive and willing to learn. One of the biggest challenges I faced at school was the death of my grandmother. My grandmother, who I call "Lola," was someone who showed me the importance of strength and caring. When I first learned that she was sick, back in the Philippines, it was hard for me to focus on my school work and on-campus commitments.

My mom wanted me to go back to the Philippines with her for a couple of weeks to visit my Lola, as she said her time was nearing an end. I wanted to go so badly, but I knew I couldn't miss weeks of school and work. I felt guilty.

A couple of months later, I was walking toward my 8:30 a.m. class when I got a call from my sister. Lola had passed away. The guilt hit me ten times harder then. I wasn't able to see her one last time, and I felt sick to my stomach. I sat in class and heard nothing of what my professor said, let alone the pop quiz we had that day. Again, my family wanted me to go to the Philippines for my grandmother's funeral, but I knew I wouldn't be able to. It was too close to final exams. I felt horrible.

Long story short, I knew the only way that I was going to be able to manage how I was feeling was to talk to my friends. Being able to talk to them, to ask them about how they deal with personal stress and student commitments, really helped. It helped me feel like I wasn't alone in this situation and that I had people to help me when I felt low. Building a community of people to help support and guide you throughout your journey in undergrad is so important. — *Julian Lao*

Living with Others

Living with roommates, housemates, and floormates can be rewarding and fun, an opportunity to expand your social circle and meet new people. But new students can struggle with sharing space with others – especially if they've never lived with anyone but family. For many Canadian students, their first year of university might be the first time they've lived in crowded conditions. Dorm life can throw students into small, often antiseptic, rooms where they suddenly have to adjust to another person's constant presence, as well as their friends, their preference in music, and their sleeping and study habits. They may also have to share bathrooms, study rooms, and lounges with other strangers.

Although this change can be frustrating at times, it's a great opportunity to learn how to set personal boundaries. If you want to study at a particular time, but your roommate has loud music playing, this is a good time to have a conversation about the kind of living space you want to share. You can also have these conversations with floormates when it comes to shared lounge and study spaces. Although these conversations can be awkward, they're important for establishing how you want to live with others. Learning how to effectively voice your concerns and expectations is a skill you'll need to develop for future living situations. When discussing how you want to live with other people, be explicit about what you want your shared space to be used for, when you like to go to bed, when you like to study, and how you like to socialize with others. Ask the people you live with what their preferences are and keep an open mind. They likely won't share all of your values, but by discussing this with them, you'll likely arrive at a compromise that suits you both, and you might learn a valuable lesson about compromising with others in the process.

GETTING HELP
How to Deal with Conflict
If you feel uncomfortable talking to others about a conflict and are unsure about how to have these conversations, there are resources available. If you live in a dorm, residence supervisors and administrators will support you in these conversations. Chatting with them might help you find the right words or another strategy to resolve the conflict. If you live off campus, try chatting with friends or family members. They might be able to help you think through the best way to frame your concerns with your roommates.

Taking Charge of Your Own Finances

For many people, going to university means being in charge of your own finances for the first time in your life. It's an exciting opportunity, but it can be challenging – especially if you've never done it before. Funds from family members are slowing down, and you have to figure out how to meet payment deadlines, balance budgets, and earn money on your own. Alternatively, you might come from a family where finances are tight. Your parents or guardians might not have been able to pay for extracurricular activities while you were growing up and can't afford to help you with tuition and student fees now. Fortunately (and unfortunately), learning to navigate these types of financial challenges is also a long-term process. Many students struggle to balance their budgets during the first year of school, whether it's discovering that they underestimated their monthly costs or have unexpected expenses. Learning the actual costs of things takes time (especially if you come from a family where you didn't have to pay for your own food, clothes, or entertainment before university).

SELF-CARE STRATEGY
Take Time to Make a Budget

One thing you can do (and something that most people avoid doing) is to sit down and make a budget for yourself. Look back through your last three months of bank statements and get a good grasp on the things that take up the largest proportion of your expenses (even before you're in university). Do you spend a lot on food? Do you like to go shopping? Do you go out for dinner or to the bar a lot?

After that, research the costs associated with going to university. If you haven't yet started, how much tuition will you need to pay, and when? Do you need a meal plan? How much is housing, and when do you need to pay for it? Are you in a program with high textbook costs? If you know some areas will cost more than others (or that you spend more on certain things than others), allocate more money to them. Also, make a calendar with important spending dates on it and write down when tuition, housing, and book purchases will happen.

After you do this, check in on your spending habits each month. (Most people are terrible at monitoring their own spending habits. It's uncomfortable to look at what you spend your money on, especially if you don't have a lot of money. But just like with anything else, the more you do it, the easier it will become.) See if you're keeping up with your timelines and if there are areas where you're underspending (i.e., spending less than you assumed) or overspending (i.e., spending more than you assumed). Change your budget to best fit your actual spending habits and then think about any lifestyle changes that you might also need to make to meet your financial obligations throughout the term.

In addition to balancing their budgets, many students juggle part-time jobs and their studies, which is a great training ground for achieving a good work-life balance after graduation. Most programs require at least thirty hours of study time per week – the equivalent of a part-time job. Course requirements can also go beyond the standard in-class time. Group meetings, extra lab time, guest lectures, and extracurricular programming can cut into time that you've set aside for employment, but you can employ simple strategies to make things easier on yourself.

Setting the Stage for Academic Success

To make it into university, you were probably one of the top students in your class. Once you arrive, however, you'll find yourself among many other high-achieving students in your program. It's important to remember that everyone else is having the same experience. Sometimes, you'll navigate these new academic challenges successfully; other times, you'll be less successful. Everyone experiences some sort of academic setback, and it could even happen in *every* year that you're at school. What sets academically successful students apart from their less successful peers is that they adapt and seek help when they need it. Your instructors, teaching assistants, and lab supervisors are all there to help you learn. All of them have years of experience in the field. Chances are they have either helped students with the same problem or have experienced the same problem themselves. If they're not able to help you, do not be afraid to reach out to other people for help until you find someone who can explain the material in a way that makes sense to you.

GETTING HELP
Financial Assistance

If you're experiencing financial troubles, here are some resources that might be helpful for you.

Federal student loans: The federal government offers a number of different loan and bursary options for postsecondary students. Visit the National Student Loans Service Centre's website for more information on specific funding opportunities.

Provincial student loans: Each province administers loans and bursary programming for students studying at local schools or out of province. Visit your provincial government's website for more information about specific funding opportunities.

On-campus financial aid: If you're experiencing a financial crisis, visit your on-campus financial aid office to receive information about potential resources. Financial assistants can help you develop budgets and will offer financial advice. Most colleges and universities also have emergency funds available to students in crisis.

SELF-CARE STRATEGY
Balancing School with a Part-Time Job

If you plan to work while in school, consider these three tricks:

- Try to find a job close to campus or your home (if you live off campus). This will help you cut back on travel cost and time, which can eat into your academic schedule.

- Try to find a job related to your field of study (e.g., as a teaching assistant, research assistant, or administrative assistant). These jobs will not only help you understand your coursework better, they'll also give you work experience, which will help you succeed in the job market.

- Try to find a job that will allow you to have a flexible schedule. Academic commitments tend to change from semester to semester. Having a workplace that understands this will help reduce your negative stress load.

VALUING AND SUPPORTING DIVERSITY

I'm a white, heterosexual, cisgender female who came from a middle-class family. My experience, though depicted as the norm in media, is not the experience of many students on campus. As a sociologist who studies mental health and inequality in education, I think it's important to consider the many pathways students take to and through university. Mental health literacy is not simply about understanding your own experiences – it's also about knowing the risks and challenges that might impact your friends and loved ones. In this chapter, you'll learn about some of the specific challenges students can face, depending on their backgrounds or how they identify. You might be one of these students – for instance, you might be the first person who has attended university in your family or you might be an Indigenous, racialized, international, or LGBT2SQIA+ student. Or, like me, you might come from a relatively privileged background. Regardless of your background, by learning about and paying attention to the needs of others, you'll be better positioned to help yourself and your friends.

First-Generation Students

First-generation students are the first members of their family to ever attend a college or university. This is a big deal! It means that they had to overcome more social and economic challenges to attend university than most other students. First-generation students bring much-needed perspectives to classroom discussions. Some students don't know what it's like to have parents who work multiple jobs; they don't know what it's like to work a job that doesn't require postsecondary education; and they don't understand the challenges associated with not having some sort of postsecondary education. First-generation students bring this experience to conversations and can help inform university programs, policies, and practices that seek to create more equitable opportunities for students. Their contributions in class push the boundaries of academic disciplines, informing new ways of thinking and innovation. First-generation students also bring a strong work ethic and academic standards that strengthen the reputation of the university and push others to try harder.

 Quick Fact First-generation students are less likely to complete an undergraduate degree than other students.

One of the challenges that first-generation students must overcome is that there may be a mismatch between the university's and their family's expectations. The research of sociologist Wolfgang Lehmann from the University of Western Ontario has shown that family members without university educations tend to highly value interdependency (e.g., working together and depending on one another), and many of the jobs available to them reward teamwork and collaborative labour. Conversely, universities tend to reward independent thinking over interdependency. Professors want students to be able to think for themselves and learn skills that will help them work as professionally independent persons after graduation. These divergent perspectives mean that first-generation students might experience a lot of stress because the values they grew up with don't hold the same weight on campus. As Lehmann's research and an article published by Marybeth Walpole in the *Review of Higher Education* in 2003 have revealed, first-generation students are less likely to complete an undergraduate degree than other students.

Another obstacle that first-generation students might have to overcome is the guilt that can come from having access to resources and employment opportunities that are closed to their loved ones. A lot of students struggle with this discrepancy. For instance, those who stay in residence might feel guilty if their family members are working multiple jobs or long hours to pay rent, put food on the table, and keep their households running.

Student Story..

I think one of the biggest challenges in my undergrad was trying to figure out what I needed to do to be successful. This involved balancing my coursework, volunteering, doing activist work, and publishing papers around LGBTQ2+ issues. I constantly felt like I needed to be doing more. I thought that if I wanted to get into graduate school, I needed to get high grades, do community work, and publish in undergraduate journals. I did all that and became an undergraduate journal editor. This ultimately worked out (I'm starting graduate school in the fall!), but it took a lot of learning and energy to understand what was needed and what was not. For someone like me, with parents who attended but didn't graduate university, I took great honour in making them proud. However, all of that came with having to socialize myself in a way to learn the "tricks of the trade" to be successful at school that other students had readily available to them. — *Andy Holmes*

First-generation students sometimes come to campus without the support and knowledge that other students have. Students who have parents or relatives who went to university have someone to guide them when they choose courses or look for help or resources. If you're a first-generation student, you might not have information and knowledge that your peers take for granted. The best thing you can do upon your arrival to campus is to seek out an academic adviser. Talking to advisers early will clue you in to deadlines, work strategies, and resources that your peers may already be using.

Because of these challenges, first-generation students tend to have more negative perceptions of university than students with university-educated parents. In her research, Walpole links their generally lower level of academic and social engagement to the fact that many maintain jobs off campus. Undergraduate tuition and the high costs of living mean that these students sometimes have to work harder than others to stay in school and keep good grades.

SELF-CARE STRATEGY
Use Existing Programs to Level the Playing Field

If you're a first-generation student and are feeling disconnected from campus life or experiencing challenges related to family or work expectations, talk to an academic adviser. They can recommend strategies that previous first-generation students have used to gain financial support and successfully navigate their undergraduate career. For example, McMaster University has peer mentorship programs that match incoming undergrads with successful upper-year students. It also has special grants and tuition subsidies for students who need financial support. Visit an academic adviser to see if your school has similar social or financial programs.

Indigenous Students

Indigenous students play a key role at colleges and universities, some of the first institutions to enter into the spirit of reconciliation and collaboration with Indigenous nations. Universities benefit from the presence of Indigenous students and faculty because they reinforce different ways of knowing and strengthen intellectual contributions that run counter to colonialist histories. These practices are essential for building trust, understanding, and knowledge throughout society. However, universities do not always reflect the values and practices of Indigenous students. Universities have a legacy of discrimination against Indigenous Peoples rooted in their historical support of residential schools, the Sixties Scoop, and ethnocentric government programming. As the calls to action and final report of the Truth and Reconciliation Commission of Canada revealed, Indigenous Peoples have experienced cultural genocide – the destruction of the structures and practices that allow groups to continue – and this history has led to their unequal treatment in all walks of life.

The residential school system originated before Confederation but was primarily active between 1876, when the Indian Act was passed, and 1996, when the last school closed. An amendment to the Indian Act in 1884 made attendance at residential schools compulsory for all First Nations children. For children at these schools, life was difficult and lonely. The buildings were often located far from their family, poorly built, and not maintained. Many students were forced to live at school with no access to their families. Staffed by religious organizations but funded by the federal government, the schools ran with little oversight. A large proportion of students experienced neglect, physical abuse, and sexual assault, and discipline was harsh. Students were punished

GETTING HELP
Well-Being Programs

In recognition of the struggles faced by Indigenous students and in response to the calls to action of the Truth and Reconciliation Commission, some universities and colleges have initiated well-being programs. For example, the University of Alberta runs cultural and emotional support programming through the First Peoples' House. It provides services and resources that reflect different Indigenous worldviews. The University of British Columbia also facilitates a Wellness Peers program that provides holistic support by promoting culturally relevant, proactive wellness strategies for Indigenous students so that they can achieve academic and personal success. Not all Canadian universities have resources specifically designed to support Indigenous students' needs, but many do. If you're having trouble finding programs, contact the Indigenous studies department on campus. They'll likely be able to point you in the right direction.

for speaking Indigenous languages, practising Indigenous cultural traditions, or trying to make contact with their families. The federal and provincial governments also passed legislation that allowed for the destruction of the schools' medical records, making it difficult to establish the number of students who perished in the schools. However, the Truth and Reconciliation Commission of Canada estimates that at least 2,040 students died in residential schools.

The trauma experienced by residential school survivors has impacted multiple generations. It has led to a distrust of colleges and universities and to social, emotional, and psychological challenges that make it difficult for Indigenous students to access higher education.

By removing an estimated twenty thousand Indigenous children from their families and communities and placing them primarily in the care of white, middle-class families, the Sixties Scoop (which actually began in the late 1950s and persisted into the 1980s) has had a similar effect. Although Indigenous Peoples resisted and continue to resist the destructive practices of the Canadian government, these practices have had long-standing impacts. And while universities and colleges have seen increased enrolments by Indigenous students in the last two decades, Indigenous Peoples are significantly underrepresented.

In addition to historical causes, this underrepresentation reflects current realities: inadequate resources in Indigenous community schools, lack of self-confidence, the absence of role models with a postsecondary education, on-campus racism, and a lack of Indigenous-focused programming. Despite these barriers, Indigenous students are keen to earn degrees. A 2005 survey by the Canada Millennium Scholarship Foundation found that 7 percent of First Nations between the ages of sixteen and twenty-four hoped to complete some form of post-secondary education, and almost 80 percent of parents hoped their children would do so.

The Truth and Reconciliation Commission has called on the federal government to "develop, with Indigenous groups, a joint strategy to eliminate education and employment gaps; develop culturally appropriate curricula; protect the rights of Indigenous languages, including teaching Indigenous languages as credit courses; and to end a backlog of First Nations students seeking post-secondary education." Universities across the country have responded with new on-campus programs.

Racialized and International Students

Just like first-generation and Indigenous students, racialized and international students make important contributions to campus life. For years, university campuses were entirely white spaces. Some schools even had quotas on the number of students from certain racialized groups they would admit. As a result, public policies and university programs did not reflect the diversity of Canada's population. Racialized and international students bring new perspectives that reflect global economies and rights movements. Their inclusion on campus is imperative if we as a society hope to thrive and grow in equitable ways.

Unfortunately, certain stressors can place them at greater risk of having mental illnesses. Although overt racism may be less commonplace on university campuses today than it was twenty years ago, it still exists. In addition to experiencing overt forms of racism on campus (e.g., name calling, vandalism, or violence), students of colour must navigate institutional cultures that deny, minimize, or superficially address racial inequalities; pressure them to assimilate to white culture or maintain racial hierarchies; and resist initiatives to bring about genuine diversity.

One way that Black students and persons of colour experience discrimination on campus is through microaggressions.

For instance, Black students have the least favourable evaluations of campus culture and report higher levels of racial discrimination, a known predictor of mental illness. One way that Black students experience discrimination on campus is through microaggressions, which University of California researchers Daniel Solorzano, Miguel Ceja, and Tara Yosso define in a 2000 article as "subtle, verbal and nonverbal acts of disregard that stem from unconscious attitudes of White superiority and constitute a verification of Black inferiority." The acts include repeating stereotypes about minority students in conversations or class or making assumptions about racialized students' worthiness to be on campus. These incidents heighten Black students' feelings of isolation and negatively affect their ability to adjust to college. Despite their reputation as inclusive spaces, campuses are often less welcoming than they're portrayed to be.

Asian students (Canadian and internationally born) are also at risk for experiencing microaggressions on campus. Comments and social cues that distinguish Asian students as "other" can increase their stress and make them feel isolated or alone. Studies show that many are at greater risk for experiencing mental illnesses than their white peers because of additional cultural pressures. For example, their families may pressure them to succeed academically so they can achieve social and economic success.

International students likewise face a host of challenges not experienced by domestic students. In particular, they're expected to meet the same rigorous academic standards as domestic students, but they don't have the same support networks. Because of this, international students are at particular risk of experiencing academic difficulties and emotional challenges.

SELF-CARE STRATEGY
Making Connections with Other Students

One way that you can overcome the disadvantages of being an international student is to try to make friends with other international and domestic students on campus. Social ties with same-country, international, and host-community students can decrease your feelings of isolation, and there are many student clubs on campus that can help you feel connected. Check out on-campus club fairs and online listings for clubs that resonate with your interests. Joining student clubs can help you make friends quickly and give you the resources you need to deal with some of the emotional and academic challenges you might experience here in Canada.

LGBT2SQIA+ Students

LGBT2SQIA+ (lesbian, gay, bisexual, transgender, Two-Spirit, queer, intersex, asexual, plus) members of academic communities have made some of the greatest contributions to knowledge. People such as Gloria Evangelina Anzaldúa, Judith Butler, Jen Jack Gieseking, Audre Lorde, Alan Turing, and Oliver Sacks are all members of the LGBT2SQIA+ community who have made or are making important additions to social theory, computer science, and neurology. As an LGBT2SQIA+ student, you, too, are an important part of the campus community.

LGBT2QSIA+ students, however, can face obstacles because of society's strict sex and gender binaries (see "FYI: Defining Sex and Gender" below). *Sexuality* refers to feelings of sexual attraction and the behaviours associated with them. *Sexual orientation* refers to a person's sexual identity in relation to the gender to which they're attracted. For example, people can identify as heterosexual (straight), lesbian, gay, bisexual, bicurious, queer, questioning, or pansexual. People who do not feel sexually attracted to others may self-describe as asexual.

Transgender is an umbrella term used to describe someone whose birth-assigned gender doesn't fully

GETTING HELP
Coming Out as LGBT2SQIA+

If you have determined that you want to openly identify as a member of the LGBT2SQIA+ communities to your friends and family members, you're likely to come up against a lot of the social, religious, and cultural pressures that kept you in the closet in the first place. This is especially true if you previously lived in an environment with limited social supports or in one that has the potential for discrimination or violence against gender-varied and gender-expansive people. If this is the case, there are a number of on-campus groups that can help you. Many people who choose to come out to their families wait until they have peer support, a sense of empowerment, and a sense of safety before they begin the process. On-campus groups can help you find these supports.

express who they are now. There are many different groups that fall under *transgender,* including (but not limited to) those who identify as transsexual, bigender, gender queer, gender questioning, Two-Spirit, and gender fluid. When Indigenous individuals refer to themselves as Two-Spirit, they could be referring to their gender identity or both their sexuality and gender identity. There are also some individuals who don't identify with any of these labels. Like other identities, the list is constantly changing to meet the needs of different groups of people.

Defining Sex and Gender — FYI

Sex, as a biological identity, is typically divided into male or female and usually determined by the presence of a penis or a vulva. The type and amount of certain hormones produced by men and women are another defining feature. Men produce more progesterone while women produce more estrogen. Although society tends to frame an individual's sex as being either male or female, there are actually a range of different identities that our physical bodies allow us to be. For instance, some individuals identify as intersex, meaning that they have physical characteristics that are not strictly male or female. Some contend that we need to expand our definitions of sex. For example, Anne Fausto-Sterling argues that we could potentially recognize five sexes instead of just two.

Another major part of our identity is gender. The concept of gender refers to the entire array of actions, behaviours, ideas, and attitudes associated with existing binaries. However, many people don't experience themselves according to a strict gender binary of being male or female. Some people feel that they ascribe to feminine traits at some times and to masculine traits at others. Sometimes, the sex ascribed at birth doesn't fit the gender that people know themselves to be. In other words, their sex doesn't reflect their gender because gender is something that is socially constructed.

Individuals who feel this way may identify as transgender, signalling that their gender identity transcends the boundaries of male or female gender statuses. Some may identify as trans-male (meaning that they identify as male, despite their sex assignment of being female at birth), and some may identify as trans-female (meaning that they identify as female, despite their sex assignment of being male at birth), while others may choose not to identify themselves in terms of these strict gender divisions. These strict gender divisions also do not fall in line with some Indigenous identities; therefore, some members of those communities may not identify themselves in those terms (e.g., Two-Spirit). Some transgender people who do not identify with the sex assigned to them at birth may choose to undergo sex-reassignment surgery. However, this is not the case for all trans individuals.

Although attitudes toward LGBT2SQIA+ people are becoming more positive, we still live in a heteronormative society. The automatic assumption for most people is that other people are heterosexual and that everyone identifies as either male or female. Because of this, LGBT2SQIA+ people still experience homophobia, on campus and off. Many campuses have therefore developed strong outreach and support programs to encourage LGBT2SQIA+ students to seek help when they need it, and all publicly funded Canadian colleges and universities have dedicated programs and resources such as clubs, safe spaces, and help centres. For example, Carleton University in Ottawa has a Gender and Sexuality Resource Centre that provides students with resources such as social spaces, sex supplies, peer-mentoring programs, referrals to community-based resources, safe(r) space training, and the second largest queer library in Ottawa. Similar services can be accessed on campuses across the country through student clubs, on-campus health centres, and counselling and well-being offices.

Transgender students face discrimination and obstacles at school that can affect their mental well-being. The discrimination they experience in primary and secondary school limits the likelihood of them even going to university, and when they do attend, they must deal with challenges such as gender-specific bathrooms and changing their identity records. Gender-specific washrooms are some of the most dangerous places on campus for transgender students, spaces where they often face verbal and physical assault and risk being questioned. Given these dangers, it's not surprising that using these spaces can be extremely stressful. To compensate, some students travel out of their way to use restrooms that are more private or avoid using campus facilities altogether.

In response to these problems, student groups across Canada have called for all existing and new campus buildings to include gender-neutral bathrooms. Many universities have begun to follow these calls to action. For example, in 2005, McGill University mandated that all new university buildings include at least one gender-neutral washroom, and preferably include at least one on every floor. The university also retrofitted all existing buildings to include gender-neutral washrooms.

GETTING HELP
Notifying the Police about Harassment
If you experience or have experienced harassment when you've tried to use an on-campus washroom, please notify the on-campus police, but only if you feel comfortable. Being approached, questioned, or threatened by anyone is not acceptable in any space. You have the right to work, study, and live in a safe place. By tracking harassment cases, university staff can take appropriate disciplinary measures against aggressive students. They can also use those cases to advocate for the creation of more inclusive washrooms and trans-literacy programming at your university.

FYI - - - - - - - *Supporting Sexuality and Gender Rights* - - - - - - -

You can help build networks to provide emotional and social support for LGBT2SQIA+ students by becoming a member of an on-campus club that focuses on sexuality and gender rights. For example, the Pride Collective at UBC provides educational and social resources for students who self-identify as LGBT2SQIA+ and their allies. It holds open meetings weekly to discuss community-action projects and resource development, and it hosts social events and safe spaces where students can study and socialize. Individual faculties also have support networks. For example, Engineering at UBC has the Gears and Queers club. You'll also find a list beginning on the next page of off-campus support groups by province.

GETTING HELP
Changing Your Gender and Name

If you would like to change your name in your school records or have a chosen name that you would like faculty and staff to use, that right is guaranteed to you as a Canadian citizen. If you encounter challenges to using your name or aggression associated with your identity at school, you should contact your university's Ombuds Office. Ombuds Offices are independent mediation services for university students. They have a mandate to confidentially and independently investigate cases where a student's rights might have been violated. Staff in these offices can help you advocate for your identity rights and give you resources for additional emotional support.

Transgender students also face challenges when they try to change their identity on school accounts. Deciding to transition from one gender to another often involves changing one's gender and name on official records and documents. Being able to do so is important both personally and legally. Having the appropriate name and gender reflects and validates an individual's identity and prevents them from being placed in uncomfortable and dangerous situations where they have to explain why they use a name that differs from their birth name or why their appearance doesn't match the photo or gender designation on their ID. The right to change one's name on school records is guaranteed to all Canadian citizens.

Quick Fact

All Canadian universities are obligated under both federal and provincial human rights codes to honour students' chosen names.

Supports for LGBT2SQIA+ Students, by Province

Newfoundland and Labrador
LGBTQ Youth Group, St. John's
A social group for lesbian, bisexual, gay, transgender, queer, questioning, and curious youth and their friends, allies, or supporters. The club offers ongoing support and monthly gatherings for anyone between the ages of sixteen and twenty-five.

Planned Parenthood, Newfoundland and Labrador Sexual Health Centre
A nonprofit charitable organization that promotes positive sexual health through education, partnership, and information.

New Brunswick
River of Pride
A nonprofit organization for and by LGBT2SQIA+ people based in Moncton.

Nova Scotia
Nova Scotia Rainbow Action Project
A social justice group that aims to help members of the LGBT2SQIA+ community build networks through public outreach, education, and political action.

prideHealth Nova Scotia
A provincially funded organization that works to improve access to health services that are safe, coordinated, comprehensive, and culturally appropriate for people of the LGBT2SQIA+ community.

Supports
cont'd

Prince Edward Island
Pride PEI
A nonprofit organization that aims to create an inclusive community through the annual PEI Pride festival and parade, ongoing social events, education, and advocacy.

Quebec
Coalition des familles LGBT+ / LGBT+ Family Coalition
A nonprofit organization that promotes family diversity, knowledge, and activism around LGBT2SQIA+ rights through workshops, activities, and community events.

Conseil québécois LGBT
A provincially funded French-language organization that works to defend the rights of LGBT2SQIA+ people living in Quebec.

Ontario
LGBT Youth Line
An LGBT2SQIA+ youth-led organization that affirms and supports the experiences of people twenty-nine years of age and under across Ontario.

Rainbow Health Ontario
A province-wide program that works to promote the health of Ontario's LGBT2SQIA+ community and improve their access to services.

Manitoba
Everyone Matters Manitoba
A province-wide program that supports LGBT2SQIA+ youth and young adults experiencing mental illness.

Rainbow Resource Centre Manitoba
A nonprofit organization that seeks to foster a proud, resilient, and diverse LGBT2SQIA+ community through support, education, and resources, including counselling, workplace educational workshops, and social support programming.

Supports
cont'd

Saskatchewan

OUTSaskatoon

An organization that provides support services and education for the 2SLGBTQ community.

Moose Jaw Pride

A nonprofit organization that provides inclusive community services and educational opportunities for all gender and sexually diverse people.

Alberta

OUTreach Southern Alberta

An outreach program that responds to the needs of the local and broader LGBT2SQIA+ community of southern Alberta and surrounding areas by providing resources, education, and opportunities to foster self-determination, civic engagement, and community partnership.

Youth Safe

A website that provides links to information and resources in Alberta for LGBTQ+ people and allies.

British Columbia

Prideline BC

A call line that offers peer support, information, and referrals for anyone in BC, Monday to Friday from 7 p.m. to 10 p.m.

QMUNITY: BC's Queer Resource Centre

A nonprofit organization that offers information, education, support groups, advocacy, and referrals for LGBT2SQIA+ youth, adults, and older adults and allies.

Northwest Territories and Nunavut

Iqaluit Pride

A public and open group for all Two-Spirit, lesbian, gay, bisexual, trans, queer, questioning, intersexed, asexual, and allies living in Iqaluit.

Supports
cont'd

NWT Pride

A community organization that supports the annual provincial pride festival, education programming, resources, and safe spaces for LGBT2SQIA+ people and their allies.

Rainbow Coalition of Yellowknife

An outreach organization that supports LGBT2SQIA+ individuals and their allies.

Yukon

Queer Yukon

Queer Yukon is a community group dedicated to building supportive networks by organizing social events for LGBT2SQIA+ Yukoners and allies.

UNDERSTANDING MENTAL HEALTH

Your undergrad years can be one of the most exciting times of your life – jammed with new knowledge, new experiences, and new friends. Learning to balance it all is part of learning to be an adult, and the stress that you feel at certain parts of the academic year can be used to your advantage. To get the most out of your education and your undergrad years, it helps to understand the relationship between stress and mental health and that there are different mental states that range from healthy to ill mental health – and not all of them are negative. What you're feeling may be negative, but the feeling could, in fact, be common. For example, you should expect to feel sad after breaking up with a romantic partner or agitated when studying for tests. But, as my own undergrad experience shows, it's also important to be aware that certain mental states are less common, and letting them continue without getting help can seriously affect your ability to function in school and in life.

Stress (the Good and the Bad)

We all experience stress, more or less, throughout our lives, and for most students it's a big part of the university experience, because you're constantly facing new experiences and not sure if you'll rise to the challenge. Fear of the unknown is typical, and it's something you'll continue to experience, even after you finish school. How do you distinguish between good stress and bad stress?

Good stress: The stress you feel before competitions or exams is causing you to focus harder on physical training or your studies, and you're excelling while still having time to be with friends and family. You feel well prepared from all your hard work, and you're excited or invigorated when you compete or write your exam.

Bad stress: You feel threatened or overwhelmed by an upcoming event, exam, or deadline. Instead of studying, your mind is wandering or you're getting lost in books, TV shows, or video games. Your eating and sleeping habits have changed. Stress can also change the way you feel about things.

Understanding how stress works and knowing that it can be managed are key tools for maintaining good mental health. People generally respond to stress with the fight-flight-freeze response. Your parasympathetic nervous system (responsible for regular day-to-day functions such as "rest and digest" or "feed and breed") takes a break, and your sympathetic nervous system kicks in. A surge of hormones such as adrenalin and cortisol make you feel more alert. Adrenalin makes your heart rate and blood pressure rise, while cortisol enhances your brain's use of sugars and tissue repair. During a stressful situation, this hormone also limits non-essential functions such as digestion, reproduction, and growth.

Quick Tip **Understanding how stress works and knowing it can be managed are key tools for maintaining good mental health.**

These changes can lead to enhanced productivity. Unfortunately, our bodies' responses don't always match the level of threat. Sometimes we produce too much adrenalin and cortisol. When the stressful situation passes, the physical response remains. Over time, high cortisol levels can have negative effects on our immune systems and digestive tracts. At other times, such as during final exams, we may feel like we're constantly under threat. This feeling can drag out our body's stress response for months.

These physiological changes can also impact our thoughts, feelings, and work habits. When you're stressed, you might find you can pay attention to one thing for a longer period of time. But you might also be forgetting about other obligations or day-to-day tasks. This way of thinking can be good when it helps us solve problems or study for a test, but it can negatively impact our relationships with others. You might be less inclined to talk to your friends and family because all of your attention is focused on the stressful event. You might be agitated by small changes or deviations from your daily routine.

The Difference between Stress and Anxiety   **FYI**

Experiencing stress and an anxiety disorder is not the same thing. Stress is a regular part of everyday life while an anxiety disorder is an overwhelming feeling of fear about everyday situations. More information about anxiety disorders is available in Chapter 8.

When we experience traumatic stress in response to a traumatic event such as an accident or physical violence, these physiological and psychological responses can be severe – trembling, shaking, a pounding heart, rapid breathing, sweating, dizziness, and trouble concentrating. These symptoms usually fade over a few days or weeks. However, it's important to know that people react differently to trauma and that we sometimes need help dealing with it.

Student Story

The biggest challenge I experienced over the course of my undergraduate degree was coping with stress. I felt it most keenly in my final semester of undergrad, because I was applying for jobs, scholarships, and graduate school. To get into graduate school, I needed to have a high GPA. I also tried to attend conferences and publish papers at the same time. I'd feel a lot of stress every time I opened my laptop to see an overwhelming number of open documents and tabs. I'd sit there looking at my screen, not knowing where or how to begin in the face of fast-approaching deadlines.

The strategy I found most helpful for managing these feelings was allocating different physical spaces for each thing I had to do. For example, I'd write papers when I was in the library on campus. I'd sit in a certain café to write scholarship applications. After that, I'd go to a different faculty building to work on my conference posters. At home, I'd set aside a specific place (my work desk) to do other schoolwork. These strategies helped me to both physically and mentally compartmentalize the work that needed to be done, breaking my deadlines into small manageable tasks. Switching up my environments also helped me streamline my focus, and I found that creating a relationship between a physical space and a mental task helped alleviate the paralyzing experience of feeling overwhelmed. —*Colleen Chambers*

The Different Mental Health States

Once you understand how stress works, it's easier to assess the state of your mental health. According to the Mental Health Commission of Canada, there are signs you can look out for to determine if you're experiencing healthy, reactive, injured, or ill mental health. Keep in mind that everyone is different, and you might not have all the signs.

Healthy. You feel calm, have a good sense of humour, can take on new things, and have no trouble focusing on daily tasks with consistency. Your grades are staying the same, and you're meeting deadlines. Waking up and going to bed at the same time is easy for you, and you feel physically well and your weight isn't fluctuating. You have no trouble keeping up with your social obligations or hanging out with friends.

Reactive. You feel nervous, irritable, sad, or overwhelmed. It's difficult to focus on your daily tasks, and you get distracted easily. You have trouble sleeping, or you are sleeping more. You aren't interacting with others as much as you usually do, and you have less drive to be physically active.

If you feel this way, you're not experiencing a mental illness or disorder but are trying your best to cope with potentially difficult everyday occurrences.

Injured Mental Health. You feel anger, ongoing sadness, or hopelessness. You have difficulty concentrating and thoughts stick in your mind. Your day-to-day activities feel more difficult than usual, and you feel tired, achy, or in pain. Your sleep is disrupted, and your weight is fluctuating. Your alcohol consumption or drug use has increased, and you're not sure if you can control it.

If you feel this way, you may not be experiencing a mental illness or disorder, but your feelings and actions have become more disruptive. You should talk to someone and ask for help. This will help you understand the distress you're experiencing and start to prioritize self-care. It will also help you maintain social contact with others and access to resources in this time of need.

Ill Mental Health. You feel excessive anxiety, panic, and can be aggressive or easily enraged. You feel numb to the experiences around you, or you no longer enjoy things you were once passionate about. You feel constant fatigue and have a lot of trouble falling asleep or staying awake. Your body is going through changes, including extreme weight gain or loss. You can't concentrate and have recurring negative thoughts. Day-to-day tasks are difficult and overwhelming, to the point where you can't perform them. You may have suicidal thoughts or intent. You are binge drinking or using drugs daily.

If you feel this way, there is a good chance you're experiencing mental illness, and it's important to seek care from a medical professional and follow their recommendations. You'll learn more about specific mental illnesses and their particular warning signs in Chapter 8.

Why Do We Experience Mental Illness?

The likelihood of experiencing a mental illness can fluctuate depending on your age, and there are different causes: genetic, biological, personality-based, and environmental.

Genetics. Many mental illnesses – such as major depressive disorder and schizophrenia – have links to inherited genetic traits, but that doesn't mean that everyone with these traits will experience a mental illness. It's true that these traits can contribute to a mental illness, but the genetic basis for mental illnesses is highly polygenetic – meaning that no one gene can influence the likelihood of you experiencing a mental illness. A combination of genes influences your risk. And genetic indicators, in turn, play only a small role in determining the likelihood of you experiencing a particular illness. In other words, you might be at genetic risk for experiencing a mental illness, but it might never express itself for you.

Biology. Most mental illnesses present themselves in early adulthood, when people are at university or just entering the work force. Research by Justin Hunt and Daniel Eisenberg at the University of Michigan suggests that female students are more likely to experience anxiety, eating disorders, and depression than their male peers. Male students, by contrast, are more liable to suffer from depression, experience substance-use issues, and to complete suicide. Although they experience a wider range of issues relating to well-being, female students are more likely to seek treatment for their mental illnesses than men and report higher rates of support from family and friends.

How Gender Expectations Can Influence Whether You Get Help

FYI

One of the main reasons that male students do not seek treatment when they need help is stigma. Male students are often more uncomfortable than their female peers with disclosing their emotional challenges to others, a feeling that puts them at greater risk for sustained mental illnesses. For men, a lot of their feelings about seeking help are tied up with socially constructed gender norms that say men are supposed to be strong and self-sufficient. They fear being punished socially for showing their emotions or talking about their emotional problems. These harmful perceptions are often attributed to toxic masculinity, the traits society associates with being a man that can cause social and individual harm. For instance, the belief that men are or should be more dominant, aggressive, and strong not only puts women at greater risk for violence and subjugation, it also harms men in their help-seeking behaviour. It suggests that strong men don't cry and don't need help. These beliefs are dangerous because they put men at higher risk for not treating mental illnesses.

Personality. Recent research by Roman Kotov and colleagues suggests that people who have neurotic (fearful) personality traits are more likely to experience negative and distressing emotions such as irritability, low self-esteem, social anxiety, and helplessness than their peers with extroverted personality traits. These emotions put them at greater risk for experiencing mental illnesses such as depression and anxiety. On the other hand, people with extroverted personality traits – who are more sociable, enthusiastic, cheerful, and uninhibited – are at greater risk of experiencing substance-use problems.

Environment. Our environments can either trigger or protect us from experiencing mental illnesses. A simple example is research by Darren Mayne and colleagues that suggests that having access to green spaces enhances our mental well-being.

More complex is the connection between our cultural backgrounds and sexuality and mental health. For instance, research reveals that the mental well-being of racialized students who suffer from discrimination can be at risk and that they may come up against emotional challenges and cultural barriers if they try to get help. A 2015 study of Vietnamese students by Meekyung Han and Helen Pong, published in the *Journal of College Student Development,* found that mental illness is highly stigmatized in those Asian cultures that attribute it to a lack of will power or self-control. For some Asian students, talking openly about feeling down or experiencing anxiety is considered shameful. They often don't feel comfortable speaking to mental health professionals who are not from the same ethnic backgrounds as themselves. In other words, they're more likely to experience anxiety and have suicidal thoughts than their white peers but are less likely to seek help.

Environmental factors can also influence the mental well-being of LGBT2SQIA+ students. Discrimination and oppression experienced during or in relation to the coming out process and other experiences related to identifying as LGBT2SQIA+ can increase some mental health risks. LGBT2SQIA+ students are significantly more likely to experience depression, anxiety, suicidal thoughts, and self-harming behaviours than their heterosexual peers. Studies of transgender individuals between the ages of eighteen and twenty-four have shown that about 20 percent exhibit symptoms of depression. The good news is that LGBT2SQIA+ students are more apt to seek out help than their heterosexual peers, who are more likely to have stigmatizing views about mental illnesses.

Adopting a Holistic Approach to Well-Being

GETTING HELP
Mental Health Outreach Programs

If you're an equity-seeking or international student, universities across the country have designed mental health outreach programs to meet your needs and help you succeed on campus. Some on-campus counselling services also include staff from a range of ethnic and cultural backgrounds. Staff in these offices can direct you to community-based resources if you don't feel that your cultural experience is represented at your university. As a university student studying in Canada, you have the right to support that suits your needs and traditions. Campus staff are equipped to help you and want you to succeed.

Keeping a healthy mind means adopting a holistic approach to well-being. In my own case, it wasn't simply the school environment that made me develop mental illnesses. Genetics, biology, and personality also played a role. Other people in my family have struggled with mental illness. I was at an age where most mental illnesses present themselves, and I tend to have a cautious, fearful personality. In short, our mental health is made up of a number of influences, and many of the causes of mental illness are things we have no control over (e.g., genetic variation or our lived environments). However, we can lessen their effect by recognizing when our mental well-being is challenged and by changing the way we think and behave.

Maintaining a healthy mind, much the same as maintaining a healthy body, requires daily care and compassion, from yourself and others. Adopting a holistic approach to mental health includes being aware of how you feel about yourself and others. This will help you manage your feelings and deal with everyday problems. There are things you can do every day to help keep good mental health. Having gratitude for the opportunities you've been given, helping others, and staying present are three that you can apply to all aspects of your university life, and you'll encounter more self-care strategies in the chapters that follow that will set you up with good habits for life.

SELF-CARE STRATEGY
Having Gratitude

Having gratitude has been linked with overall improved well-being and mental health. Unfortunately, it's not always an easy thing to think about. We all get caught up in the hustle and bustle of everyday life and sometimes forget to take stock of things we are thankful for. It's also tough to have gratitude when you're not feeling great. But feeling gratitude doesn't mean you need to be grateful for everything in your life, all of the time. Instead, try to think about one or two things a day that you're thankful for or appreciate. You could recognize these things by writing them down in an agenda or journal. Recording these thoughts will help you get in the habit of identifying things you appreciate. And you'll have a nice record to reflect on when times are tough.

Research shows that helping others not only benefits them – it makes people feel like they can handle new challenges and solve problems on their own. They see more value in their own actions and feel better about themselves. There are a lot of ways you can help others, and they don't need to be big. They can be simple things such as helping family members with household tasks or pitching in to help a friend move or make something. If you want to help out on a bigger level, try seeing what volunteer opportunities are available in your community. All of these things can help you feel more connected and better about yourself.

SELF-CARE STRATEGY
Being Mindful

Being mindful can be quite simple, so long as you remember to do it! Set aside a few minutes each day to stop and feel. Either stand still or sit down. Then think about what you're experiencing with all your senses. What do you see around you? Are you in a classroom or the campus grounds? What do you smell? Is it cut grass, or is it chalk? What are you touching? Are your feet touching soft grass, or are you sitting on a hard bench? Can you taste anything? Maybe you're chewing gum or drinking coffee. Taking note of your current environment will help you focus on what you're doing and thinking in the current moment.

Another simple strategy is writing down the things you hope to get done in a day and why you want to do them. Being present is an exercise in bringing attention and focus back to yourself and whatever you're doing.

Being mindful and living in the moment can be hard, particularly when you're a university student and life is moving at warp speed. Being present means being aware of your environment, the tasks you have to do, how those tasks make you feel, and what kinds of outcomes you want. It also means letting go of negative experiences in the past that may prevent you from moving forward in the present.

FOUR

MEETING ACADEMIC HURDLES HEAD-ON

Undergraduate life can sometimes feel like a nerdy version of *American Gladiator.* Just when you think you've managed to climb one academic hurdle, new challenges pop up, ready to knock you back down. This week it's midterms; next week, multiple essays are due; and for week three it's labs and assignments. Your friends want to hang out, and your parents are complaining about your grades. Sometimes, the whole routine gets exhausting. It makes you feel like graduation is impossible, and to top it off you're not even sure if you like your program. Keep in mind that many of the challenges that you're facing are not new. Others have experienced them too. In this chapter, you'll learn about common academic challenges and how to cope with them.

Dealing with Poor Grades

It's not unusual in first and second year for students to experience a drop in their grades. Adjusting to campus life can be stressful, and this stress will usually impact grades negatively. However, while a drop of 10 to 15 percent in first-year studies is not unusual, grades that fall below a program's threshold by more than 15 percent of your regular GPA are of concern. Almost every program on campus has a mandatory average that students must maintain to remain enrolled. If your grades fall below that average, you run the risk of being cut from the program. Your university also has a standard average that you must maintain to keep your admission. If you notice your grades starting to slip, you need to talk to someone sooner rather than later. Many students wait until they're failing or until the university intervenes to discuss their academic progress. By then, it's usually too late to put your academics back on track. As soon you see a change in your grades, you need to seek help.

A drop of 10 to 15 percent in your first-year studies is not unusual. But if your marks don't return to normal after that or they fall below average, seek help immediately.

The first step in getting your grades back on track is to talk to a teaching assistant (TA) or professor in the courses you're not doing well in. Faculty never want to see students fail, and there is no shame in asking for help. When I was an undergrad, I had a terrible time in my statistics and math courses. I got so frustrated with my inability to understand what was going on that I skipped lectures and readings. I fell behind everyone else. Fortunately, I had a fantastic TA who noticed my struggles and offered to chat with me. She explained that she had also had trouble understanding statistics and showed me how she learned the material. I realized two things. First, sometimes the way instructors teach won't resonate with our own learning style. Second, most professors or TAs wouldn't be where they are today if they hadn't asked for help at some

point in their own academic careers.
Having difficulty with some subjects
is common. Asking for help can get
you back on track.

Visit your professor or TA during
office hours to discuss your grades
and your study habits and to get
their advice on how to improve in
their class. *Do not* go into their office
demanding better grades or insinuat-
ing that their teaching is terrible or
the reason you're not doing well in
their course. It will not go over well.
Even if an instructor's teaching style
doesn't fit with your learning style,
you need to talk to them to learn
how to adapt to meet their expectations. However, if there is a major gap
between their academic expectations
and their ability to teach the material, you might need to talk to the TA.
Chances are the TA will be grading
the assignments for the course and
can explain what you need to do to
improve your grades.

If you have talked to your professors and TAs and are still having
trouble meeting academic expectations, then it's time to talk to an

GETTING HELP
The Accommodations Office

If you have specific learning
needs, an academic adviser can
refer you to an accommodations
office, which will customize
your program of study, exams,
and assignments to suit your
needs. For example, if you have
a known learning disability –
such as a written output disorder,
which affects the speed at
which you're able to write, or a
medical condition such as Type I
diabetes, which might require you
to take a break during an exam
to test your blood sugar – the
accommodations office can help
you get more time for exams.
An academic adviser will also
help you assess which program of
study fits best with your skill set.
Maybe you really love a field of
study but struggle with the course
work requirements. If that's the
case, an adviser can talk to you
about other programs that match
your interests and abilities.

academic adviser. Every university in Canada has academic
advisers. Part of their responsibility is to refer students to
study groups, tutors, and workshops on campus. They can

also help identify why a student is struggling academically. In some cases, students have additional learning needs that must be accommodated to help them succeed (e.g., a diagnosed learning disability).

FYI ---------------- *Imposter Syndrome* ----------------

Experiencing academic challenges can strike a blow to your self-esteem and make you feel like you don't belong. Most people who attend university received top marks in high school but at university find themselves in the middle of the pack, surrounded by other high-achieving students. Feeling unsure about yourself is typical. It means you're invested in a process and are concerned with the quality of your work. If you think you know everything, you won't continue to seek out new knowledge, educate yourself, and expand your horizons. However, when these feelings become debilitating or limit you from trying new things, they're called "imposter syndrome."

Imposter syndrome is a pattern of thoughts that students sometimes get stuck in. If you suffer from it, you doubt your accomplishments and have a persistent internalized fear of being exposed as a fraud, as I did when I was a student. These thoughts are obstacles because they can undermine your study habits and academic goals. Thinking you aren't capable can discourage you from studying and keeping up with your readings, bad habits that will only reinforce your negative perception of yourself. Negative thoughts can also stop you from applying for scholarships, programs, and other academic awards. Positive thinking is important to your academic success. Everyone experiences setbacks; the challenge is not letting them get to you.

If your confidence in your abilities is lagging, talk to your friends, an academic adviser, an instructor, or a TA. They'll give you some perspective on the difficulties you're experiencing and the common challenges of your program. They'll likely also give you tips on how to overcome some of the feelings that you're experiencing. If your teachers and friends can't help you with these feelings, you should consult a mental health counsellor. There are also online resources, such as impostorsyndrome.com, that can help you better understand what imposter syndrome is and the challenges that you may be facing.

Managing Your Parents' Expectations

Many students' parents try to give their children every opportunity to do well in school. Despite your parents' best intentions, they might be placing too much pressure on you to succeed. A number of studies have demonstrated that excessive academic pressure from parents can affect the mental well-being of students, which can in turn hamper academic performance.

To maintain a healthy relationship with your family when it comes to your academic performance, discuss the issue openly with them, but only if you want to. You are not obligated to share your grades with your parents, even if they're paying for your tuition. A university cannot legally share that information with them without your written consent. Many parents don't know what first-year averages are at universities or the grades you should be getting in specific courses. They probably don't know how students generally perform in biochemistry courses or what grades are expected for you to stay in your program. Finding out what the averages are (from your department or a faculty member) may help your parents keep your grades in perspective... if you want to talk to them about it.

SELF-CARE STRATEGY
How to Talk to Your Parents about Your Grades

If you choose to talk to your parents about your grades (you don't have to!), open the conversation by asking them what they hope to achieve and why they expect you to achieve those grades. It's important that both you and your parents contribute to the conversation. One side coming up with solutions is not an effective strategy to resolve a conflict. However, keep in mind that this conversation might be extremely difficult. There are a lot of emotions tied up in your academic progress. If you find this conversation too overwhelming, try breaking it down into smaller parts by having multiple conversations that touch on only one part of the problem. Over time, these small conversations can help you find solutions and resolve the conflict.

First, talk to them about how difficult some of your courses are. Next, discuss class averages with them and where you stand in comparison. If you're below the class average, you can brainstorm strategies to increase your grades. Next, talk about things that worked and things that didn't. Breaking the conversation down into smaller parts will help both you and your parents feel like you're effectively helping each other.

Another strategy you can use is called the **DEAR MAN** approach. It's an acronym for the steps you can take to ask for something (even if it's just understanding) or to say no to a request.

Describe the situation or issue factually. Do not make any assumptions about or interpret the issue. Example: "I got 68 percent on my statistics midterm. The class average was 70 percent. I studied one hour per day for a week."

Express how you feel about the situation. Example: "I'm feeling really disappointed. I studied very hard, and this was the best I could do. It's hard for me to see you upset with me about this."

Assert what you want and say no to things you don't want. Example: "Could you please stop talking about my grades?

It would help me if I could spend less time doing chores during midterm week or not attend family events when I should be studying."

Reinforce your requests by sweetening the deal or spelling out the consequences. Example: "If I can have more time to focus on my studies, I'll be more likely to improve my grades for next time" or "If you don't use more supportive language, I'll find it hard to maintain a positive relationship with you."

The MAN portion of the approach describes how to enact the stages of conversation.

Be **mindful** by focusing on your goal and not letting your emotions take control. You might inadvertently place blame on someone or say something hurtful. It's okay to sound like a broken record.

Appear confident by making sure that your body language, posture, and expressions are clear and assertive. But don't be aggressive. Face the person you're talking to and maintain eye contact with them when they're speaking.

Negotiate by being open to compromise. If you're willing to give a little, your parents or guardians will be more likely to give a little, too.

Problems Meeting Deadlines

If your lower grades mean you're having trouble keeping up with your school work, consider taking a reduced course load. Many students consider this a sign that they can't cope with the rigorous demands of academic life. That's not true. Many extremely successful students reduce their course loads to manage their academic commitments. Fewer classes means more time to complete assignments and readings and more time to seek help from instructors if needed. You'll also have more time to appreciate your studies and actively engage with class materials.

Keep in mind, though, that reducing your course load will prolong your undergraduate degree. It might not fit with your immigration status as an international student, and it may affect your student loans or housing eligibility. Taking fewer courses also means that you might not meet scholarship requirements and might have to take summer courses. Taking these classes can cut into your budget by reducing your ability to hold a full-time summer job. If you're having trouble managing your time, you should talk to an academic adviser to see if a reduced course load is right for you. If it isn't, there are other options that won't inhibit your ability to complete your program.

Developing Good Study Habits

Developing good study habits is one of the best ways to set the stage for academic success. You might think that how you studied in high school will carry over into university, but studying for university courses is much different. You'll be expected to engage in both comprehensive and critical learning.

Comprehensive learning is common in high school and when studying for a test. It involves reading a paper or textbook to find the answers to preconceived questions. For example, you might read through a text wondering, *How is this concept or term defined? What actions characterize this process? In what year did this event occur?* Sometimes, when people practise comprehensive reading, they make note of key terms, ideas, or definitions. This type of reading is often linked to memorizing key points for a test.

By contrast, critical learning stresses evaluation over memorization. This type of learning starts when you ask questions about the reading. For example, you might ask yourself, *Why did the researchers present their argument this way? Why is this example relevant to the main argument? Why did they use this research strategy? What other conclusions could be drawn from these findings?* You read critically when you try to reconstruct the logic of the writer's argument and approach to the research question.

Certain fields of study rely more heavily on one type of learning than the other. However, you'll be expected to engage in both types of learning in every program. When you sit down to complete your readings and assignments, think about which learning style you're engaging in and what types of questions you should be asking yourself before you start.

When you do this, it's also helpful to have a general understanding of how to complete certain readings. Undergraduate students tend to have the most difficulty understanding academic articles. Most are used to reading textbook chapters that clearly outline and define the learning objectives and terms. Academic journal articles can be less straightforward. When it comes time to sit down to read one, there are two approaches to consider. First, you can try to complete your reading efficiently, meaning don't waste valuable time reading superfluous portions of the text. Focus on the sections most pertinent to the subject. Second, you can also try to read more effectively by identifying and understanding the key points.

How to Dissect a Journal Article   **FYI**

The following tips are for articles in the sciences or social sciences. Articles in the humanities do not tend to follow this formula, but the general approach still applies.

1. *Start with the abstract.* The abstract is written like a directions guide. It outlines the main issues or ideas.

2. *Jump to the end of the article.* Research discussion and conclusions sum up the article. If the article isn't an assigned reading, they'll help you decide if the article is worth your time.

3. *Go back to the introduction.* Read the introduction and think about how the author approached the research problem. This should make the findings clearer.

4. *Move on to the literature review.* The literature review, which typically follows the introduction, reveals how the author situates their research in existing fields of study and discusses other studies that might be relevant.

5. *Complete the remaining sections.* Read the sections that remain and take note of how the findings were obtained and measured and how they relate to the author's argument or theoretical framework.

Learning to read efficiently and effectively are skills that take a lot of time to develop, and some readings will require more time to complete than others. Everybody reads at a different pace, and depending on your faculty or subject matter, you might have to spend more time studying than your friends in other programs. Reading a research article comprehensively might take anywhere from thirty minutes to an hour (or longer). Textbook chapters are normally a bit longer than journal articles and should take between an hour to an hour and a half to complete. The length of time it takes will also depend on the material and the chapter length.

When you sit down to complete your readings, you should take notes, but don't mindlessly write down everything. Make note of ideas that come to you while you read the text, either in the margins or as edit notes on a PDF. Your notes can be comments or questions. They'll not only help you remember key passages when you reread the text – they'll put you on the pathway to developing your own ideas.

You can also highlight or underline key passages. Doing so for arguments, equations, definitions, findings, or conclusions will make it easier for you to remember the material and come back to it. If you find yourself highlighting too much text, try using brackets or comments instead. Or try drawing pictures and logic diagrams that explain a step-by-step process or theoretical pathway. For instance, logic diagrams can connect and explain ideas or systems. A logic diagram might look something like this, with *A, B,* and *C* representing the development of different theories, ideas, or processes.

Finally, after honing your reading and note-taking skills, reassess how you study for exams. For many students, writing exams can be extremely challenging and stressful. Some courses require students to write short essays or solve complicated problems. There are a number of things you can do to prepare, which will only increase your confidence:

- *Know what's on the exam.* What parts of the course will the exam cover? Check the syllabus, ask your peers, and talk to the TA or professor. Will the exam be cumulative (covering all course material up to the test date)? And what readings are mandatory?

- *Know the format.* Different types of exams require different study habits. Studying for multiple-choice exams usually requires comprehensive-learning rather than critical-learning techniques. The opposite is true for short-answer or essay questions.

- *Give yourself time.* Do not cram the night before. Effective learning, which is based on doing all the readings and then reviewing your notes, takes time. Two of the most effective study strategies are spacing and testing. Spacing involves reviewing an item then taking a break from it. Nicholas Cepeda and fellow researchers note in their 2006 article in *Psychological Bulletin* that testing means coming back to an item you've reviewed to determine whether you understand and remember it.

- *Check in with your professors.* You might find that there is course material that you're not confident about. Don't be afraid to ask your professor or TA about it. They'll give you the correct answer, and you'll be more likely to remember it. As a caveat, do not inundate your professor with unnecessary questions. If the answer is something you can easily find by reviewing the syllabus, asking a friend, or searching the internet, pursue those options first. The questions you bring to your professor should be specific to content learning.

- *Make questions, ask questions.* A great way to study is by making mock exam questions from your materials. You might find that as you do this you stump yourself on the answers. That's okay! Reach out to your peers or teachers to answer questions you're hung up on. Having a discussion about material is a great way to further your understanding of it.

What If You Hate Your Program?

What happens if you're doing everything right – you're getting good grades and balancing your studies with a social life and a job – but you hate your program? Many students feel pressure to stay in the program they started in first year. Sometimes, they worry that if they change their program people will think that they've failed or had to drop out. What most students don't know is that 30 percent of students change their field of study. Changing your program can help you find a field of study that matches your interests, which will often translate into doing better in school.

Student Story..

In high school, I identified as a keen, active environmental activist. I helped organize and participated in rallies, student groups, and conferences, and being an environmentalist became an important part of my identity. When I entered university, it seemed an obvious choice to declare a minor in environment and society. It took me three years into my undergraduate career to realize that the courses required for the minor were not going well. I found the material difficult to understand, and I often didn't look forward to attending the classes. Receiving poor grades at the end of the term didn't help. It was a stark contrast to my sociology classes, which I was engaged, inspired, and passionate about. I came to the tough decision to drop my minor in environment and society.

It was difficult to accept that a key part of my identity in high school had changed sharply in university. I eventually came to terms with the fact that identities are constantly changing, and that it was okay to accept them. Some of my peers discovered they didn't enjoy their area of study, but they didn't have another area to fill the void like I had with sociology. I consider myself incredibly fortunate to have found sociology to complete my academic identity. —***Emily Chan***

If you feel disconnected and unmotivated in your program of study, talk to an academic adviser in your department or faculty. They might be able to tell you if what you're feeling is simply symptomatic of the courses you're taking. Many first- and second-year undergraduate courses are very broad. You likely won't delve into more nuanced material until third or fourth year. If this is the case, a department adviser might refer you to courses better suited to your interests. They might also suggest work-learn opportunities – such as being a research assistant, a co-op student, or a department administrative assistant – that can help you become more engaged in your field.

An adviser can also refer you to another program that better suits your needs. They usually have excellent connections on campus. Chances are that if you're feeling disconnected from your program, other students have felt the same way. Sometimes advisers have helped students with problems like yours and can send you down a similar path. If your program-specific adviser can't recommend other programming, schedule a meeting with a faculty-wide or university-wide adviser. These advisers are more familiar with the range of programs at the university and might be able to point you in a new direction that you'll find more satisfying. You can also try taking a course from a different program to see if it appeals more to your needs or interests.

If You're Considering Grad School or a Professional Program

Are you thinking about going to graduate school or a professional school or program (e.g., a master's program or law, medicine, or dentistry)? Great! Grad school is an opportunity to build on your previous learning experiences and to do independent research. However, like dealing with bad grades, thinking about applying to grad school should happen sooner rather than later. It will take a lot of time, money, and energy, on top of your regular academic requirements.

Applying to grad schools can also be really exciting. You're applying for something that will likely bring you closer to achieving your career goals and will help you achieve the life outcomes you desire. Keep in mind that there are many different postgraduate programs to choose from, and they're not the same at every school (even if they have the same name). Different departments and faculties have their own specialties and aims, so when you choose to study at a specific program or school, make sure that your aims align with theirs. Go online and review the areas of focus of the postgraduate program that you find interesting.

The best advice I ever received when applying for grad school was to put love into my application. Believe in yourself and work hard to construct an application that you're proud of. If you do this, and ask for help from others (e.g., grad students, faculty members, academic advisers), there is a good chance you'll achieve your goals.

If you apply for grad school and are not successful, no worries. This happens to a lot of students. When you're putting together your application, you should consider a Plan B – professional work related to your field of study that might help you in your application process the following year. Some graduate schools are more willing to accept students who have applied multiple times or who have pursued related work in the meantime. They know that these students are serious about pursuing postgraduate work and that they'll come to the program with real-world experience. Pursuing your Plan B, if you don't get into grad school, can also help you figure out if grad school is the right place for you. Sometimes, students start jobs and realize that the work they're doing is better than anything they could have pursued in grad school or after.

SELF-CARE STRATEGY
A Recipe for a Less-Stress Application Process
If you're thinking about going to graduate or professional school, here are some things to consider:

- *Start the process as soon as possible.* Depending on the program, applying for graduate school can take anywhere from four to six months. Completing applications can be a lengthy process because you'll likely need to complete standardized tests (e.g., the LSAT, MCAT, or GRE), write multiple statements of intent (one for each program you apply to), and compile multiple reference letters from faculty.

- *Keep track of deadlines and expectations.* Some programs have multiple application deadlines (e.g., payments are due a month before the actual application), but most Canadian postgraduate application deadlines fall in December or January. American postgraduate applications are usually due a bit earlier. Each graduate program also has different expectations for grade-point averages, previous professional work experience, extracurricular work, and publication histories. Some graduate schools require a specific grade or higher on standardized tests. To help you keep track of everything, set up a spreadsheet.

- *Finding a supervisor.* If you pursue a research-focused postgraduate degree, you'll have a supervisor, a faculty member who oversees your progress and helps you with your research. When you apply to a program, you suggest who you would like to work with. To figure out who fits best with you, check out some of the research being done by faculty members. Find one whose research matches your interests. Ideally, they should also have the same work style and personality. You can figure this out by asking the department to put you in contact with students who worked with that faculty member.

You should also contact the potential supervisor. They'll recognize your name when they review applications, and you might gain a better understanding of whether you'll work well together.

- *Write a personal statement, if required.* Many students think their personal statement should reflect their personal interests and life story. It should not. Your personal statement should outline your academic abilities and experiences, research or professional aims, and why the program is a good fit for you. Ask a graduate student or a faculty member in the field to review it.

- *Gather references.* If you're applying to a research-focused program, you should ask for letters from tenured professors whose research aligns with your own interests. Reference letters from sessional instructors won't hold as much weight as those from full-time faculty members. When you ask faculty members for a reference, they should be the instructor of courses you did well in and familiar with you and your academic aims. Before asking for letters, develop a relationship with your professors by visiting them occasionally during office hours. Some professional programs might require a reference from previous employers. These letters should be from managers or business owners in your field rather than lower-level employees. Lastly, don't simply ask if someone can write you a reference letter. Ask if they can write you a good reference letter! To aid them, provide them with an outline of the program (a link to the website works), a draft of your statement of intent, your resume or CV, and a transcript.

The basic message that I'm trying to convey is that your undergraduate career will be full of new experiences and opportunities. Most of time, they'll be exciting, but sometimes they'll seem overwhelming. The tips and self-care strategies outlined here will give you the personal and professional skills needed to meet these hurdles head-on and soar.

MAKING TIME FOR FRIENDS AND EXTRACURRICULARS

Studying and getting good grades is important, but meeting new people and creating new social networks is also a big part of the university experience. I thought I'd have no problem making friends when I moved away for school because I'd had no problem making friends back home. But I failed to realize that my friends back home had been with me all through school. We had built our relationships over time. Thinking that I could move onto campus and start up similar relationships in only a few weeks wasn't realistic.

Making friends happens easily for some people but not for everyone. Some people are simply too shy to reach out. Others have just arrived from another country. Still others live at home or off campus and have existing friendship networks off campus. Regardless of your situation, it's important to keep in mind that having friends who share your experiences is essential to your mental health and well-being. This chapter explores some of the things you can do to build better relationships on campus – from joining clubs, to volunteering, to extracurriculars. Along the way, it includes tips and strategies to help keep your social life in balance with your studies so you can have a truly well-rounded and fulfilling university experience.

Making New Friends and Feeling Like You Belong

It's hard to feel lonely when you feel like you belong. Feeling like you're a member of a campus community can help protect you against mental illnesses such as depression or anxiety, and it can help improve your grades. Having meaningful connections with others means having an emotional and academic support system. You can talk to others about how to choose courses, manage deadlines, and deal with conflicts or problems with students or professors.

These connections won't happen overnight. Universities place a lot of emphasis on successful integration into campus life, but the research on belonging shows that developing a feeling of belonging is a process that differs from student to student. Be patient and understand that different people make friends in different ways. Some students enjoy getting together in large groups while others tend to prefer one-on-one relationships. Think about the type of social connections you like to share with others and find opportunities to develop them. If you like being around large groups of people, invite people to go to a sporting event or concert with you. If you're not into big group gatherings consider inviting people for coffee or a meal.

Connecting with others can be a lot simpler than you think. Research shows that having something small in common – such as liking the same music or sports team – can be enough to spark a strong social bond. Try new things, learn what you like, and try to form social networks around those interests.

Student Story..

As a commuter student, I found it difficult to find friends at school. I came from a very small high school, and few of my friends ended up going to the same university as me. My friends that did end up going to the same school didn't have the same schedules, and I rarely got to see them. I felt like the strong connections I had with people before university were fading, and I had no one on campus to hang out with.

By the end of my first year, I was determined to meet new people and build new connections on campus. I decided to volunteer in some on-campus leadership initiatives, such as peer advising and first-year orientation. In my second year, I signed up for my department's undergraduate society. These opportunities were really helpful to me because they meant that I could see my new friends in class, meetings, and social gatherings multiple times a week. I enjoyed volunteering so much that I later became the co-president of my department's undergraduate society for two consecutive years. It was through my involvement with these groups that I met some of my best friends and bonded with others through coursework struggles and our shared laughs in meetings. *—Cecilia Federizon*

Sports and Clubs

You can make connections with others who share your interests by joining a sports team or club. Some Canadian campuses have over one hundred student clubs and sports teams centred on different ethnic, cultural, social, and physical interests. When you join, you'll automatically meet people who share your interests.

You can also join a team or club that has nothing to do with your interests or athletic abilities. Sometimes, trying something new is a great way to make new friends. Most clubs and teams host introduction nights and regular social events. If you don't feel comfortable going to one of these events on your own, find someone in your classes or from residence to go with you. They can help you feel more comfortable trying something new (because they're doing something new too), and you get a chance to know them better.

Quick Tip

Research shows that having something small in common – such as liking the same music or sports team – can be enough to spark a strong social bond.

For some students, entrance to university is dependent on their participation in varsity sports programs or the performing arts. Taking part in extracurricular activities is healthy for many students, but being part of multiple clubs and sports teams can easily turn into a long-term juggling act. If you take on multiple extracurricular activities, you might need guidance on managing high academic standards, social relationships, and activity schedules.

SELF-CARE STRATEGY
Balancing Team Sports and Study Time

Some sports teams have TAs and academic advisers to help students manage their grades and athletic commitments. If you have access to these resources, use them. These people are available because the school knows it can be difficult for you to manage your schedule. Take their help and learn how to effectively manage your time. If you're not on a varsity team and don't have access to these kinds of academic resources, sit down and map out how much time your sports and clubs are taking up compared with your classes and social life. If you have trouble balancing these three things on your own, talk to an academic adviser. They can help you develop strategies to manage your commitments.

Greek Life

If your university has them, joining a fraternity or sorority is a great way to make new connections. Being part of "Greek life" automatically connects students to a network of people with similar interests and programs of study. Some fraternities and sororities also have chapters with memberships that span decades and host social events that give you the opportunity to network with alumni. But beware: a major downside of Greek life is the time commitment it requires. Fraternities and sororities support their social networking opportunities through an endless stream of events, fundraisers, and planning meetings.

Research by Elizabeth Armstrong and Laura Hamilton, sociologists who specialize in the social behaviours of university students, shows that while these networking opportunities are great for students from high socio-economic backgrounds, commitments to Greek life are not as helpful for students from middle or low socio-economic backgrounds. Belonging requires a lot of money (e.g., membership fees) and time. For students from less privileged backgrounds, the costs tend to outweigh the benefits of networking. They also end up "paying more for the party" because their grades suffer, and they don't have the same networks to draw on after graduation when they're searching for jobs. If you're considering becoming a member of a fraternity or a sorority, consider the costs and whether they outweigh the benefits.

Quick Tip

Students from low socio-economic backgrounds end up "paying more for the party," so think carefully before joining a sorority or fraternity.

Volunteering

Students can meet new people and earn work-related experience by volunteering. Universities partner with community groups that offer volunteering opportunities to their students, including placements in hospitals, nongovernment organizations, and conservation groups. Helping out with a student theatre group, organizing intramural sports programs, or joining faculty-specific student groups can also teach you organizational skills as you meet people with similar interests.

Search out opportunities to volunteer by thinking about the types of groups you'd like to help and then see if your university has a partnership with an organization dedicated to that group. If it doesn't, there could be community groups that you can join simply by emailing them. Helping others is a good way to help yourself, and campus life offers many opportunities.

Coping with and Overcoming Loneliness

Many students struggle to connect with others during their time on campus. If you're having trouble making friends, talk to your existing friends or family members. The relationships you had before coming to university are still important. Lean on them if you need social and emotional support. You can tell them that you feel scared about meeting new people or trying new things. They might be able to help you think of strategies to meet new people that fall in line with your own personal interests. If you don't feel comfortable talking about your social challenges with your friends or family members, counsellors can help you think of safe and comfortable strategies for meeting others and feeling less lonely.

As a take-home message, don't get frustrated if you don't have a lot of friends or a sense of belonging in your first year at university. Feeling connected to your campus community is something that takes time. It also takes some investment of time and energy to find others who share your interests. However, if your first year at university starts to mirror my own (i.e., you're spending all your time alone in your room feeling frustrated with your situation), you likely need to talk to someone. Be good to yourself. Think about your situation with some compassion, recognize your challenges, and ask for help if you need it.

GOING OUT AND STAYING IN

Television and movies often have us think that going to university is all about partying, drinking, and staying up until the wee hours of the morning. For a selected few, this might be what campus life looks like. However, research published on addictive behaviours among college students has revealed that most students party only occasionally, and some students don't at all. Don't go into school thinking that your social life needs to look like the movies. In this chapter, I'll help you figure out what type of social life you want to have on campus and how you can make it work for you, including dealing with peer pressure, navigating new sexual relationships, and dealing with sexual assault and violence. Being a member of your campus environment is not only about going out and having fun – it's also about supporting others and helping them have healthy and happy social lives too.

Balanced Partying

Going out and spending time with friends is a large part of undergraduate culture, and partying can be fun, but it can cause serious problems for some students. For example, some students have trouble balancing party life and their academic responsibilities. The usual workweek can go out the window. Tuesday isn't just Tuesday, it's Tequila Tuesday! Thursday isn't just Thursday, it's Thirsty Thursday! If you want to party, there are endless opportunities, almost every night of the week. However, you can overcommit yourself and start to use substances in ways that are unhealthy (see Chapter 8). Staying out late, feeling exhausted, and having hangovers can eat away at your time and energy. A lot of students think they can balance work and play, but if the majority of your time is dedicated to social activities, your academics will suffer.

SELF-CARE STRATEGY
Balancing Your Social Time with Your Studies

If you think that you might be spending too much time going out or partying, take a step back and think about how often you're getting together with friends. Measure that against your academic commitments. If you spend more time doing social things than academics, you might need to re-evaluate your schedule. If you're spending too much time partying, try to set some boundaries for yourself. It's good to get together with friends and unwind, but do it when it won't take away from your school work.

Try scheduling get-togethers only once or twice a week and plan out when you'll work on school assignments or study for tests. If you don't have an agenda or calendar, now is a good time to get one. Physically writing down when you're socializing and when you're doing school work will help you visualize where you're spending the most time and how you need to prioritize your commitments. As you do this, remember that you'll need to recalibrate your schedule every once in a while. When it's midterm season, you might not be able to hang out with your friends as much as you want. However, you might have more time to spend with them at the beginning of each semester. If you plan your time right, you can have a great social life and good grades too!

Peer Pressure

Some students can feel disconnected because they're not as into going out and hanging out with people as their friends are. Going out, drinking, and meeting new people can be fun for some, but for others it might go against their personal beliefs and values. If you don't believe in drinking or dating, you can still have a good time and participate in campus life. There are students on campus who share your values and interests. Find the clubs and organizations that best suit your social needs. You can also try planning your own social activities with small groups of friends. You don't always have to go to the bar, drink, or hang out on campus. Maybe playing sports, attending an event, or going out for dinner will better suit your social needs.

Quick Fact — Most students party only occasionally, and some students don't party at all.

Sometimes, your friends will pressure you to spend more time with them. This can be especially challenging if you're living in residence or in off-campus housing with people who have active social lives. If your friends are more socially active than you are, that's okay. The undergraduate experience is different for everyone. Some students like to get together with friends a lot, some only occasionally. Get together with your friends only when you want to. If you feel pressure from your friends to get together more frequently than you want, have a conversation with them about when you want to hang out. Similarly, if your friends are doing things that you're not into – including having parties or inviting a lot of people back to your place – you should tell them that too. Most people will respect a friend who clearly states when and where they want to hang out. However, keep in mind that you'll need to state these things explicitly. A lot of people miss subtle social cues about other people's social preferences. If your friends don't respect your preferences, you might need to state them again or have conversations with others who do understand your needs. The sooner you can all be on board with one another's likes and dislikes, the sooner you'll all enjoy university life.

Quick Tip

If you're feeling overwhelmed by social life on campus and don't want to do anything with others, try talking to someone about the way you're feeling.

GETTING HELP
Feeling Overwhelmed

If you're feeling overwhelmed by social life on campus and don't want to do anything with others, this might be a sign that you're in a reactive state of mental health. It's common for students to need some time to adjust to changes and find their place at university. However, if you're feeling nervous interacting with other students or if you're spending the majority of your time alone in your room or at the library (by choice, not because of assignment deadlines), it might be helpful to talk to a counsellor. Overcoming these fears can be extremely difficult on your own. On-campus counsellors are trained professionals who can help you find the tools you'll need to feel more comfortable at school.

Let's Talk about Sex

Many high school students can't wait to go to university so they can start new relationships without their parents' supervision. Sex should be good, healthy, pleasurable, meaningful, and fun. Engaging in sex with a consenting partner is not shameful. It should be a positive experience, and you shouldn't be afraid to have conversations about it. However, navigating the feelings of others is no cakewalk. For many students, university is the first time they'll explore different sexual experiences, and it can be difficult to understand what the other person (or people) is thinking. Having sex doesn't have the same meaning for everyone, and sometimes students feel pressure to engage in sexual behaviours that they're not ready for. For some, having sex can go against their personal beliefs and values. But being sexually active is often seen as a way to find intimacy and a sense of connection at school. However, this can be extremely hard for students whose personal values do not coincide with certain sexual behaviours. Because most undergraduate students want to establish connections with others, many find it hard to say no to sex without worrying that they'll be socially isolated. Unintentionally pressuring someone into engaging in sexual activity can have long-term emotional and psychological consequences, for both the victim and the person who went too far.

If you're thinking about having sex or feel uncomfortable with certain sexual behaviours, it's important that you talk about them with your partner. Although these conversations can feel awkward at first, they're extremely important. These discussions are about giving consent and understanding the feelings that others have around intimacy. They'll also protect you from unintentionally pushing your partner into engaging in actions that they may not be comfortable with and can help you set boundaries around what types of intimacy you want to have with others.

Consent, or Yes Means Yes **FYI**

If you're in a relationship or plan to be intimate with someone, it's the responsibility of the person who initiates the sexual activity to establish consent. It's never the other person's responsibility to say no to being sexually assaulted. Legally, the initiator must ensure that they have received a clear yes.

Here are some ways to make sure that you receive and maintain consent:

- Consent means saying yes to sexual activity. *Yes* must be freely given and communicated clearly. Consent must be free from coercion, deception, or abuse of power or authority. Alcohol or drugs can affect someone's ability to think and communicate clearly. A person cannot legally consent if they're drunk or high.

- You have not received a yes if the other person is on a date with you, accepted a drink, flirted with you, wore something revealing, had sexual experiences with you before, or has a "reputation."

- Someone has consented if they say yes or, even better, "Yes, please!" Some questions you might try asking include "May I ___ ?," "Do you like it when I do this?," "Do you want me to keep going?," or "I really want to ___ your ___ . Do you want me to?"

- Getting consent shows that you respect your partner, and it gives everyone a chance to agree on what they want to do.

- If you do not get sexual consent, you may end up doing something the other person doesn't want.

- Even if someone says yes, they have the right to change their mind. If they change their mind, stop what you're doing.

- *No* means no, and there are other ways to say it, including "Not now, maybe later," "I'll think about it," or "I'm not sure."

- Not responding also means no.

Sexual relationships can also be complicated by ideas about intimacy, and these ideas can put you at risk for contracting sexually transmitted infections (STIs). Although university-aged individuals have the highest rates of infection, they're often unlikely to get tested or seek treatment. In a study of sexually active undergraduate students in the Maritimes, more than half had never been tested for STIs, and more males than females reported never being tested. The Public Health Agency of Canada recommends that sexually active individuals under the age of twenty-five get tested once a year. Most universities offer a range of sexual health services to promote healthy sexual behaviour and to prevent sex-related illnesses. This means that your campus has free STI testing, education, and contraceptives available on request. If you're sexually active, take some time to visit your campus's student help services office to discuss how you can keep yourself and others healthy.

Sexual Harassment and Violence

Canadian universities have beefed up awareness campaigns about consent and sexual misconduct on campus. A number of high-profile sexual misconduct cases have been reported in the media, and organizations and social movements focused on sexual rights, including Take Back the Night and #MeToo, have led to much-needed social conversations. In 2014, St. Mary's University in Halifax, Nova Scotia, investigated its Frosh Week celebrations after an Instagram post by the university's student orientation leaders featured a group chant celebrating nonconsensual, underage sex. Similar cases have been investigated at UBC, Queen's University, and Western University. In response, most campuses now run annual campaigns to raise awareness about consent and sexual violence. These campaigns include conversations about how to discuss intimacy with partners, what consent means, and how to engage in safe sex. Many campuses have also created protocols for addressing sexual violence on campus and are working to improve their student support centres so that they can help students who have experienced sexual violence.

Awareness has increased but sexual violence remains a serious threat for students. Female undergraduate students are significantly more likely to be sexually victimized than their male peers. In fact, Bonnie Fisher notes in a 2000 report, *The Sexual Victimization of College Women,* that about 20 to 30 percent of female students will experience some type of unwanted sexual contact. And an article published in 2016 in *Social Science Journal* by Lee Johnson, Todd Matthews, and Sarah Napper notes that transgender students are more liable to encounter sexual violence than women. LGBT2SQIA+ students

GETTING HELP
Reporting Sexual Violence
If you experience sexual violence, please contact health services and the police as soon as possible. If you're not comfortable contacting the police, visit your hospital emergency room or health services to talk to them about reporting the incident. If you do not feel comfortable accessing help through these resources, please speak to or visit your on-campus sexual assault centre. These places operate according to survivor-centric principles and provide non-judgmental advocacy and support. Staff help victims get informed and weigh their options, and they provide referrals to other resources. You have the right to a number of supportive options and the time to choose which option is best for you. Reaching out and asking for help can be extremely difficult, but there are services and supportive people available to help you in your time of need.

are also significantly more likely to experience sexual violence than their heterosexual peers. Although some groups encounter sexual violence more than others, there is a good chance sexual violence is something that will affect either you or your friends at some point in your undergraduate years.

If you're a friend of or know someone who has been a victim of sexual violence, your support is important. Sometimes, people who have been victims of sexual violence need others to talk to or lean on for emotional support. Although you're not a counsellor, you can help them by just being there and telling them you believe them. If you feel you're unable to help or need guidance on how best to provide support, your on-campus counselling services or crisis centre will have information for you.

DOING IT ALL AND STILL HAVING TIME FOR YOU

Self-care **is a** term that gets thrown around a lot these days. Many companies use *self-care* to sell products or to advertise their brand. However, you don't need to buy a trendy yoga mat, start visiting juice bars, or take regular bubble baths to practise it. Some of the best self-care practices are absolutely free! Self-care strategies are any actions that you take in your day-to-day life to maintain your well-being, and you've already encountered a number of them throughout this book.

To maintain good mental health, there are a lot of other activities that you can incorporate into your day-to-day life. You can engage in regular exercise, keep a healthy and balanced diet, maintain a regular sleep schedule, and do a hobby or go outside more. In this chapter, you'll be introduced to research-based practices to help you care for yourself.

Regular Exercise

Physical exercise is one of the best ways to improve your emotional health and can include any physical activity that is planned, structured, and repetitive, including running, walking, swimming, cycling, hiking, dancing, doing yoga, or weight training at the gym. Unfortunately, if you're feeling low, one of the last things you want to do is to get up and get moving. Physical activity tends to occur less in people with depression. However, research shows that consistent exercise – even as short as fifteen minutes, three times a week – is significantly associated with improved mental health. Exercise can help you manage your well-being by improving your physical, physiological, and emotional health.

Research shows that consistent exercise – even as short as fifteen minutes, three times a week – is significantly associated with improved mental health.

In terms of the physical and physiological benefits, regular exercise can help reduce blood pressure, improve cardiovascular health, and help with weight loss. It also increases endorphin levels (hormones that our bodies produce to help us endure pain and stress). Production of these hormones is associated with the phrase "runner's high," which refers to the feelings of euphoria and relaxation that follow an intense workout. Being physically active can also help you gain muscle mass and improve your balance, both of which are linked positively to self-esteem. When you're active, your body is capable of doing more things, and this can help you have a better appreciation for yourself. Exercise changes your body's physical and physiological condition in ways that promote positive mental health. In studies of individuals with depression, regular and moderate to high-intensity exercise was shown to lessen depressive symptoms. If you're experiencing emotional troubles, getting up and moving around can help your body physically respond better to stressors.

Regular exercise has also been shown to help people manage their emotional and mental health because it serves as a form of distraction. Both high- and low-intensity workouts such as running, yoga, and Tai Chi have been proven to help people feel reduced symptoms because they give them a "time out" from their feelings. This is something that a lot of gyms and fitness centres have already picked up on. Most gyms play upbeat music and locate large television screens near workout stations. They distract you from the demands of your workout and the negative feelings that might have followed you into the gym.

Exercise can also make you feel good about yourself and your abilities. Mental health researchers call this feeling the mastery or self-efficacy effect. As study published in *Preventive Medicine* in 2011 showed that individuals who engaged in six hours a week of moderate to vigorous aerobic exercise had a significant increase in their feelings of self-efficacy. Self-efficacy is generally that feeling you have when you feel like you can succeed at any task you undertake. Higher rates of self-efficacy are related to lower rates of depression and a higher likelihood for task completion. Both high-intensity and low-intensity exercise can help you improve your feelings of self-efficacy. Scheduling exercise (like going for a walk or a run) and keeping to your planned workout can improve these types of feelings and reduce any stress you might be experiencing.

If you're experiencing prolonged emotional troubles, regular exercise might help you alleviate some of your negative thoughts. However, it won't completely change the way that you think about things. To overcome negative thoughts, you should visit counselling or health services.

SELF-CARE STRATEGY
Exercise, but Don't Overdo It!

If exercise is already a regular part of your routine, it might be tempting to skip workouts during busy parts of the academic year, but resist the temptation. Keeping it up will help you perform at the highest level.

If you want to use exercise to improve your mental health and overall well-being, try engaging in physical activity in a new setting (away from home) or at a gym with music and other activities going on around you. This will help you take your mind off your stressors while giving you the psychological and physiological benefits of exercise. If you don't like working out in a gym or don't have the time to exercise outside of your home, try listening to music while you exercise. This will help you disconnect from some of the thoughts and feelings that you've been carrying through the day.

But don't overdo it! Remember that exercise isn't a cure-all, and it can be abused. A moderate amount of exercise is beneficial, but don't submerge yourself completely in an exercise regime. You might end up physically injuring yourself. Sometimes, people can also use exercise to avoid their feelings or as a replacement for an addiction. Unfortunately, using exercise in this way can reinforce negative thoughts (e.g., it can strengthen problematic perceptions about yourself). If you're someone who struggles with an eating disorder or a substance use problem, talk to your doctor or a health care professional about how to take on a healthy, regular exercise routine.

A Healthy, Balanced Diet

When people talk about the importance of eating a healthy diet, they're usually referring to the nutritional benefits that eating lots of fruit and veggies has on our physical health. However, a healthy diet is also extremely important for maintaining good mental health. There's an inverse association between diet quality and common mental health disorders, meaning that people who eat healthier foods are less likely to experience mental illnesses. Conversely, people who don't eat a healthy diet are more likely to experience mental illnesses. For example, a high consumption of meat and processed foods has been linked to an increased risk of experiencing depression, anxiety, psychosis, and bipolar disorder. Unhealthy diets can also exacerbate pre-existing mental illnesses. The research of Fernando Gómez-Pinilla, a professor in the Department of Integrative Biology and Physiology at the University of California, notes that eating too many of these types of foods – which tend to be high in sugar, trans fats, and saturated fats – can negatively affect our ability to process thoughts and learn new tasks.

There's an inverse association between diet quality and common mental health disorders, meaning that as you eat healthier foods you're less likely to experience mental illnesses.

One way to maintain or build a healthy mind is being conscious of your food choices. A growing body of research demonstrates that people who eat a diet that consists of some fish, multicoloured fruits and vegetables, and nonprocessed foods have a reduced risk of experiencing mental illnesses. Our everyday diets do not contain all the vitamins and nutrients that we need to stay healthy, and many people are actually deficient in important nutrients – Omega-3 fatty acids and vitamin D – that help with brain function. These deficiencies have been linked to cognitive impairments, depression, bipolar disorder, and schizophrenia. One of the best ways to maintain or reintroduce these two fundamental nutrients to your diet is to consume fish that live in deep cold water, such as salmon and trout. Adults who are not pregnant should eat at least eight ounces or two servings (one serving is the size of a deck of cards) of fish a week. If you don't like eating fish, another way that you can get these nutrients is through dietary supplements. Fish oil and vitamin D are both available in pill form. However, before you start taking any health supplements you should check with a health care professional to see if they're right for you. Certain supplements can cause adverse reactions if you suffer from allergies or if they're mixed with other medications.

Another way to improve your mental health is by eating a diet that consists primarily of nutrient-rich multicoloured foods. Eating these foods will also reduce the temptation to eat heavily processed foods, which contribute to poor mental health.

SELF-CARE STRATEGY
Changing Your Diet

There are a lot of ways you can change your diet to support your mental health. Try starting the week off by planning your meals. Think about how you can incorporate a range of different fruits, vegetables, and proteins into your diet. Consider how many meals one recipe will afford you (i.e., if you make a pot of soup, will that supplement your lunches and dinners for several days?). Consider whether portions of your dinner recipes can be eaten as leftovers for lunch during the week. This strategy can help you avoid buying unhealthy foods on campus and keep your food budget in check. If you're the type of person who gets bored eating the same thing every day, try making a large batch of chili, curry, or soup and then freezing small portions. Freezing food will help you avoid waste and give you healthy dinner options on evenings when you're too busy to cook.

If you're worried that you don't have the cooking skills required to prepare your own meals or that buying more fruit and veggies will be too expensive, there are online resources you can consult. For example, YouTube has basic cooking videos that will teach you how to properly chop vegetables and cook rice, meat, and pasta. Online food blogs can help you plan weekly meals on a student-friendly budget. Blogs and sites such as BudgetBytes and CookingLight give price breakdowns for recipes so you can see if they'll fit with your spending goals.

Another way to learn new cooking skills and save money is to cook with friends. Inviting your friends over or organizing a cooking party at someone else's house is a great way to learn new techniques and recipes. Chances are, you have family members who know a thing or two about cooking. If they live nearby, ask them to spend an evening together, buying groceries and cooking a meal. This will help you learn new techniques, share some of your food costs, and build new food traditions.

Unfortunately, living on campus can limit your opportunities to cook for yourself. Fortunately, most dining halls provide students with a wide range of healthy-eating options. Although the all-you-can-eat ice cream bar and poutine station can be extremely enticing, try to make a conscious effort to avoid these kinds of overprocessed foods. Instead, try to become more acquainted with the cafeteria's fresh foods and healthy-eating options. Making your cafeteria tray as fresh and colourful as possible will help you get the nutrients you need to keep a healthy body and mind.

The way we think about food can also impact our overall mental health. It's quite common in Western society to consider eating simply a daily necessity – a perfunctory task we do to break up the day. However, thinking about our meals as a time when we can come together with others to nourish our bodies and minds can have positive implications for our mental health. Research demonstrates that activities such as preparing meals ourselves, eating at home with others, and sharing our lunchtime with friends and colleagues are socially rewarding and beneficial for maintaining overall mental well-being.

Getting Enough Sleep

Getting enough sleep can be difficult. If you regularly pull all-nighters to complete assignments, celebrate with friends by going out, and then sleep in to compensate for later bedtimes, you might not be getting all the sleep you need. Getting enough sleep is one of the most important elements of self-care you can practise as a student, and sleeping in class doesn't count! How well you sleep and how many hours you get each night can impact your school work and overall well-being. For example, a 2000 study by Ann Williamson and Anne-Marie Feyer shows that going seventeen to nineteen hours without sleep is equivalent to having a blood alcohol content of 0.05 percent! Even worse, if you pull an all-nighter, meaning that you've been awake for over twenty-four hours, that's the equivalent of a blood alcohol content of 0.10 percent. Under these conditions, it's unlikely that you'll be able to complete assignments or exams to the best of your ability. And, even if you've managed to get a full night's sleep following an all-nighter, you probably won't have enough energy or feel refreshed enough to get through the day. Going long periods without sleep or not getting enough sleep is associated with increased risk of cardiovascular problems, digestive issues, and mental health conditions.

Quick Fact Going seventeen to nineteen hours without sleep is the equivalent of having a blood alcohol level of 0.05 percent.

If you would like to improve your sleep habits, there are two things you should consider: (1) your sleep quantity, and (2) your sleep quality.

Sleep quantity refers to the number of hours of sleep you get each night. The average adult requires seven to eight hours of sleep daily. However, if you're an athlete or are working to maintain your physical fitness, you may need between seven and nine hours of sleep to help your body repair itself. Just like your muscles, your brain also needs time to rest and repair from all of the activities you have done each day. *Sleep quality* refers to a number of things, including how deeply you sleep, how easily you fall asleep, and how easily you wake up in the morning.

SELF-CARE STRATEGY
Tracking Your Sleep Habits

To ensure that your body and mind are getting the rest they need, try keeping a sleep journal next to your bed for two weeks. Track the time you go to bed, the time that you get up each morning, and any extended periods of wakefulness during the night. This will help you figure out if you're getting enough sleep each night.

Getting the right amount of sleep is an important part of maintaining good health because it impacts your circadian rhythm. Your circadian rhythm is basically your twenty-four-hour internal body clock that determines when you feel most sleepy and most awake. Maintaining the circadian rhythm is critical for the production of essential bodily hormones throughout the day. If you're awake and asleep at different times each day, your body's hormone production can become irregular, making it difficult for you to fall asleep and be awake when you want. The best way to keep your circadian rhythm in check is to make sure that you wake up at the same time every day. Even if you go to bed late some nights or plan to get more sleep on the weekend, set your alarm for the same time each morning. This will help ensure that when evening rolls around you'll feel tired enough to fall asleep easily and feel refreshed when you wake up the next morning.

To measure your sleep quality, you can also include some notes in your sleep journal about how well you slept the night before. For example, did you wake up multiple times? Did you have trouble falling asleep? Did you have trouble waking up in the morning? How refreshed did you feel in the morning? Tracking these things will help you gauge not only how many hours of sleep you get each night but also how well you sleep through the night.

If you're keeping a regular sleep schedule but not getting the quality of sleep you want, there are a few tricks you can try to help feel more rested:

- *Make your bedroom a cave.* The ideal sleep environment is a cool, dark, quiet, and comfortable space. If your bedroom is too warm or too bright, these conditions can harm the quality of sleep you're getting each night.

- *Keep your sleep space tidy and separate from your work space.* If you have a lot of items on your bed, floor, and around your room, they might impede your ability to focus on your sleep (rather than the chores you've been avoiding). Although you likely lack the space to set up a desk outside your bedroom, try not to do your school work in bed, and move your computer out of your room at night.

- *Avoid consuming substances that affect sleep.* Caffeine has a lengthy half-life (three to seven hours), meaning that it acts as a stimulant in our bodies long after it's consumed. Avoid drinking coffee, tea, cola, or energy drinks after lunchtime.

- *Avoid consuming alcohol before bed.* Although most people think that alcohol consumption will help them sleep better, because it generally has a sedating effect, it actually has the opposite effect. Alcohol metabolizes differently than other food and drink, and this process can significantly disrupt your sleep.

- *Avoid bright lights and screen time before bed.* Computer, television, tablet, and cellphone screens all produce a type of blue light that mimics natural sunlight and can trick our brains into limiting the production of melatonin (the primary hormone responsible for feeling sleepy). Data suggests that even one to two hours of electronic use before bed can negatively impact melatonin release. If you need to use these devices before bed, try dimming the lighting and downloading applications to inhibit the amount of blue light they emit.

If you try all these things and still have difficulty sleeping, discuss the issues with a health care professional. They can help you determine if there is an outlying health issue impeding your sleep and suggest other strategies to remedy it.

Make Time for Hobbies

Aside from exercising, eating well, and getting enough sleep, having a hobby is helpful for maintaining your overall well-being. A hobby can be anything you love to do, including drawing, running, dancing, skating, reading, playing board games, hiking, building things, or volunteering. Whatever you choose as your hobby is not important (so long as it's healthy and legal). What is important is that it makes you feel good.

Quick Tip

Hobbies can help you develop a stronger sense of self-worth.

Taking time to engage in a hobby or another leisure activity can improve your well-being in a number of ways. First, research shows that hobbies help people cope with and prevent stress. A 2000 study on women's mental health, for example, showed that hobbies can take people's minds off stressful life events, contributing to lower levels of anxiety and depression. Conversely, a lack of involvement in leisure activities or hobbies has been linked to higher rates of anxiety and depression.

Hobbies can also help you develop a stronger sense of self-worth. For example, when exams or assignments don't go to plan, these setbacks can be interpreted as a personal failure, a feeling that can negatively affect how you think about yourself and your capabilities. Taking a break from your studies to do something you love can help remind you of your skills and talents. It can also help you put things into perspective. By stepping back and doing something else, you can see that there are other things in life that are important and that making mistakes doesn't necessarily mean that you're fundamentally flawed or incapable.

Doing hobbies, especially hobbies such as sports or games that involve other people, can also help you build friendships. Research by Anne Passmore and Davina French has shown that group hobbies promote social inclusiveness and encourage self-expression. But even solitary hobbies such as gaming or photography can help you build friendships if you join local or online communities based around your particular interest.

SELF-CARE STRATEGY
Developing a Hobby

If you don't have a hobby but would like to take one up, think about all the things that you enjoy doing. Do you like being outdoors? Do you like reading? Do you like making things or working with your hands? A hobby doesn't need to be related to your school work or the types of things that your friends enjoy doing. The important thing is that it's something that you enjoy doing.

If you're interested in a particular hobby but don't know how to go about starting it, talk to friends or family members who do that activity. If you don't know anyone who does it, look for groups online or in your local community. With the help of the internet, information on almost any hobby is available for free. Figure out what you like, do some research, and spend some time doing things that bring you joy. Even trying out new things might lead you to a new pastime or interest. "Variety is the spice of life" is an old and wise saying.

Enjoying Nature

Getting outside is one of the easiest ways to practise self-care. Unfortunately, more than half of the world's population now live and work in settings that limit their contact with the natural environment. And most school work takes place inside, at a desk in front of a computer screen. But you don't need to spend a lot of time in nature to enjoy it benefits. A 2010 study showed that even ten to five minutes in a green space can help improve a person's self-esteem and mood, regardless of the intensity of the activity or location. The same study showed that getting outside has positive mental health outcomes, including reduced symptoms of stress, anxiety, and depression.

SELF-CARE STRATEGY
Get Outdoors

There are a number of strategies you can use to take a break from technology and enjoy the benefits of being outdoors:

- *Go for a walk.* Sometimes, we overlook the simplest self-care solutions. Going for a walk around the block or in a park is a great way to de-stress. It helps your brain take a break from overstimulation and helps you focus on things outside of school work. You can do it rain or shine, and most of the time you'll find that when you finish your walk you feel more energized and refreshed. If you want to get outside more, try challenging yourself to go for a walk after dinner or in the afternoon once a week.

- *Eat lunch outside.* Get outside and enjoy the fresh air. As an undergrad, you spend so much of your time at a desk or table working, why would you want to spend your free time doing the same thing? Try asking your friends if they want to eat lunch outside when the weather is nice. If the weather is not so nice, grab a snack or hot chocolate and go for a walk.

- *Choose outdoor physical activities.* Going to the gym or taking a yoga class is a great way to stay active. Try to

> build on these activities by cross-training outdoors with activities such as stair climbing, running, cycling, or hiking. Instead of always doing indoor yoga lessons, try finding ones in your community that are outdoors.
>
> • *Plan outdoor activities with friends.* Outdoor activities with friends will take you away from your everyday activities stressors, and they usually cost a lot less (if they're not free) than doing indoor activities such as going to a movie, restaurant, or bar.

Going outside can help you maintain your overall well-being in a number of ways. It will help you get away from stressful environments and maintain your physical health, and it will increase the likelihood of social interaction. If you need more incentive to spend time outside throughout the week, most campuses have outdoors clubs and sports teams that organize recreational activities on weekends and evenings. Interest-based clubs – such as gardening, drawing, and photography – also tend to host outdoor events. By joining one of these organizations, you'll be combining two self-care strategies – taking part in a hobby you love and being outdoors!

Celebrate Your Achievements

Life moves fast, and more often than not we don't take time to acknowledge when we've done something right and too often focus on things we've done wrong. You made it to university, you enrolled yourself in courses, and you're trying to make new social connections. Celebrate your achievements. Recognizing successful moments is extremely important because marking them in some way will validate your experiences at university and give you a sense of accomplishment about your work.

The achievements you celebrate don't need to be big. Getting an academic award or being accepted into a selective program are great achievements and definitely deserve celebration. However, these things come infrequently for most students. Allow yourself the time to observe smaller victories. Getting a good grade on an assignment, winning an intramural sports event, making a new friend, or pushing yourself outside your comfort zone are all achievements that should be recognized. You don't have to spend money or publicize it on social media. You can do those things if you feel comfortable, but taking a break from your daily schedule to do something for yourself, like going for a walk or doing an activity that you enjoy, can also be gratifying. What's important is that you've recognized that you've achieved a goal (no matter the significance) and taken time to acknowledge it.

RECOGNIZING THE SIGNS OF MENTAL ILLNESS

The mental health tips and self-care strategies scattered throughout this book are intended to help you maintain a healthy mind and succeed in all aspects of university life – academic, social, and physical. Self-care is a big part of mental health literacy, but so too is knowing what type of help is available if you suspect you're experiencing a mental illness. In Chapter 3 you learned how to distinguish between the different types of mental states on a continuum from a healthy mental state to an ill mental health state. This chapter opens by letting you know what to expect if you recognize the warning signs in yourself and decide to seek help from a professional. Fear of the unknown often prevents people from seeking treatment when they need it most. In my own case, when I was first struggling with mental illness, I didn't know what would happen if I talked to others about it. Maybe the university would identify me as someone who couldn't cope with my coursework and kick me out. Or maybe my friends would reject me because they wouldn't trust me anymore or think I was weak. None of these things happened. But the fear kept me from getting help sooner.

The remainder of this chapter outlines the types of mental health illnesses that might affect you. It's not meant to be used as a tool for self-diagnosis. The goal is to describe each one generally – from anxiety to suicide – so you can recognize some of the behavioural signs and seek help to manage and prevent them from negatively impacting your life or the lives of your friends.

Visiting an On-Campus Counsellor or Doctor's Office

If you suspect that you're no longer in a healthy mental state and want to visit your on-campus counselling centre or doctor's office, here's a typical scenario.

First, they'll ask you for identification and a health card (if you're a Canadian citizen). If you're an international student or don't have a health card, the administrator will ask for alternative identification or other health documents.

Second, you'll either fill out a form (or questions on an electronic tablet) or will be asked questions about your medical history and how you're feeling. Remember, care providers will not pass judgment on your situation. They simply want to figure out the best way to help you. Give them as much information as you can. None of this information will make it into your academic records and it will remain confidential.

Third, you'll be taken in to your appointment. After asking about your physical and mental well-being, the counsellor or doctor might ask about your goals for the visit and what you hope to get out of it. You might not have a clear idea about what you want, or maybe you just want to feel better. That's okay. If you do have a clear idea about the kind of solution you need, talk about it. If you don't, say that you're unsure.

Fourth, after assessing the challenges you're experiencing, they'll provide you with different care options. They might provide a single option or multiple options, including one-on-one counselling or therapy, group therapy, medication, or work sheets, readings, and activities. Some of these suggestions might not fit with what you think you need. Keep in mind that different solutions work for different people. Just because you don't think it will work doesn't mean it won't be helpful. Be open to their suggestions.

Fifth, you might need to speak to a counsellor, therapist, or doctor multiple times to get the right treatment. Mental health, like your physical health, takes time. If you break your leg and go to hospital, the doctor will need to assess the break, put a cast on it, and give you some pain medication. The healing process will likely involve physical therapy. Mental health care professionals work in the same way. They make assessments, provide immediate care (if necessary), provide medication (if necessary), and give you follow-up work that will help make the feelings you're experiencing less troubling in the future. Visits with a counsellor or therapist can span weeks or months. Your care provider might suggest that you get involved in community-based activities or change your lifestyle to promote good overall health.

As mentioned before, there are four degrees of mental health you'll experience in your lifetime (e.g., a healthy mental state, a reactive mental state, an injured mental state, and mental illness). Your doctors or other health care provider might not use this terminology during your visit. However, being able to recognize the state you're in will help you figure out what kind of help you need.

Anxiety Disorders

Feeling anxious is something we all experience at times. Many students get nervous before an exam or when they have to speak in front of the class. However, anxiety disorders are different from everyday feelings of stress or discomfort. They're illnesses that occur when certain fears become excessive and challenge multiple areas of your life, such as school work, employment, or relationships with friends and family members. There are four different types of anxiety disorders that undergraduate students tend to experience:

- generalized anxiety disorder
- social anxiety disorder
- panic disorder
- obsessive compulsive disorder.

Acquainting yourself with some of the common characteristics of these disorders will help you assess your own thoughts and behaviours or understand what others who have them are going through. These disorders are chronic, meaning they last a long time and can become progressively worse if they go untreated.

Generalized Anxiety Disorder

Generalized anxiety disorder is excessive worry that occurs for the majority of days over the course of several months. A key characteristic of this illness is that sufferers feel that their worrying is uncontrollable. People with generalized anxiety disorder will experience most of the following symptoms:

- feeling restless or on edge
- feeling easily fatigued
- having difficulty thinking or experiencing moments of mental blankness

- being easily irritated
- experiencing muscle tension, typically in the neck or shoulders
- having trouble sleeping or sleeping more than usual.

Social Anxiety Disorder

Social anxiety disorder involves feelings that are similar to generalized anxiety disorder. However, the feelings of anxiety and fear are more focused on social interactions or performance situations. People with this disorder fear being exposed to new social situations or situations where they feel others will judge them, and these situations invariably induce intense anxiety or distress. They might experience some of the symptoms of a panic disorder or have a panic attack if they're exposed to certain social situations. Sufferers also know that their fear is excessive and unreasonable, but they often don't feel like they can control it. As a result, they tend to avoid social situations that cause distress. These avoidance behaviours cause significant harm to the sufferer's personal routines, academic performance, and relationships with others.

Panic Disorder

Panic disorder involves reoccurring and unexpected panic attacks. They can be triggered by stressful situations, or they can happen without warning. If someone is having a panic attack, they'll usually experience at least four of the following:

- increased heart rate or heart palpitations
- sweating
- shaking or trembling
- shortness of breath

- chest pain or discomfort

- nausea

- dizziness or light-headedness

- feelings of detachment.

People who suffer from panic attacks fear having reoccurring attacks and might avoid situations that induce them. They also tend to worry about the implications of an attack, including fear of losing physical control of themselves or having a heart attack.

 Jokes about OCD downplay how debilitating its symptoms can be for people.

Obsessive Compulsive Disorder (OCD)

Many people make jokes about people having OCD. They'll say that a friend has OCD if they keep their desk or dorm room clean. But these jokes downplay how debilitating OCD symptoms can be for people. According to *Psychiatry,* obsessive compulsive disorder has two parts:

- Obsessions: "intrusive, recurrent, unwanted ideas, thoughts or impulses that are difficult to dismiss."

- Compulsions: "repetitive behaviours, either observable or mental, that are intended to reduce anxiety caused by obsessions."

Some of the repetitive behaviours that people with OCD engage in include handwashing, organizing and reorganizing objects, and checking on things (e.g., testing that lights or appliances are turned off multiple times). Having OCD can be devastating for sufferers because these behaviours can fill up an hour or more of their day, and they can sometimes cause themselves physical harm. For students, these behaviours can be extremely difficult because they also tend to impede social interaction and school work.

Depression

Depression is not simply about feeling sad. It's a medical condition with a range of symptoms that can affect people emotionally, physically, behaviourally, and cognitively. About one in five Canadians will experience depression at some point in their life, and undergraduate students are more likely to experience depression than the general population.

The most common type of depression is major depressive disorder. This mood disorder is characterized by feelings of hopelessness and a lack of focus on a daily or almost daily basis. These feelings last for most of the day and for at least two weeks. These are some of the most common characteristics:

- feeling sad, empty, or hopeless

- irritability or frustration

- loss of interest in most or all regular activities, including sex, hobbies, and sports

- sleep disturbances, including insomnia or sleeping too much

- tiredness and a lack of energy

GETTING HELP
National Anxiety Resources
Anxiety Canada is a registered charity that provides information about different anxiety disorders: what they look like, how they're experienced by different age groups, and different management strategies. It provides access to online videos and audio conversations about living with anxiety, along with a free, downloadable cognitive-behaviour-therapy application to help people manage their anxiety.

- reduced appetite and weight loss or increased appetite and weight gain

- slowed thinking, speech, or body movements

- fixation on past failures or self-blame

- trouble thinking, concentrating, or making decisions

- poor performance or attendance at school.

GETTING HELP
National Depression Resources

The federal government has online resources that provide definitions for different types of depressive disorders and tips for minimizing your risk of experiencing serious problems related to depression. These resources also provide information about and links to nationally supported mental health supports.

The Canadian Mental Health Association's website has information on how to recognize the symptoms of depression, the types of people it commonly affects, and the different treatment options available. It also includes links to community-based supports, depending on your location in Canada.

If you've experienced some of these symptoms for more than two weeks, it's important to contact a mental health counsellor or doctor for help. Depression is a serious mental illness that shouldn't go untreated. Students with depression are significantly more likely to have suicidal thoughts (see below) and to attempt suicide.

Eating Disorders

Sometimes, stress can negatively impact how people eat and how they think about their bodies. Being around a lot of people and living in a highly competitive environment can also make students develop unrealistic ideas about themselves, including an overconcern about weight gain, which can lead to problematic eating behaviours. Students who have these feelings sometimes develop eating disorders – unhealthy eating patterns that negatively impact their physical and mental well-being. The two most common eating disorders are anorexia nervosa and bulimia nervosa.

The Differences between Anorexia Nervosa and Bulimia Nervosa **FYI**

Anorexia

- refusal to maintain body weight at or above a minimally normal weight for one's age and height

- avoidance of food, social situations with food, or food-related rituals

- a change in the way one's body weight or shape is experienced or a denial of the seriousness of a low body weight

- lack of menstruation for at least three cycles.

Bulimia

- recurrent (at least twice a week) binge-eating episodes (e.g., eating, in a short period of time, an amount of food larger than most people would eat during a similar period of time or feeling like you can't stop eating or control how much you're eating)

- engaging in self-induced vomiting or using laxatives, diuretics, enemas, or excessive exercise to compensate for overeating

- a change in the way in which one's body weight or shape is experienced.

Most people with eating disorders do not fit all of the criteria (e.g., they may still menstruate but avoid eating and have a lower-than-average body weight). However, if you do meet some of the criteria (e.g., you avoid eating or are compensating for eating by vomiting or taking medication), please talk to a health care professional or a counsellor.

GETTING HELP
National Eating
Disorders Resources

The Canadian Mental Health Association's website has information on how to recognize the symptoms of different types of eating disorders, including anorexia nervosa, bulimia nervosa, and binge-eating disorder. It also explains who these disorders commonly affect and the different treatment options.

The National Initiative for Eating Disorders is a nonprofit organization that works with caregivers, patients, and practitioners to promote research-based treatment methods for eating disorders. It includes information on different types of eating disorders and research-based intervention methods.

Eating disorders can have extremely negative long-term consequences on physical health, including permanent hormonal imbalances, digestive tract damage, and cardiovascular disease.

Substance Use Disorder

Many students choose to experiment with drugs, and when they're enjoyed responsibly these "feel-good" things in life can have benefits, but they can also lead to problems if they're not managed properly. Students sometimes become unexpectedly dependent, and dependency or addiction can cause serious physical, mental, academic, and social problems. This section of the book uses a harm-reduction–based strategy for discussing substance use. Other agencies or institutions may not use approaches that fall in line with the suggestions listed here. However, in keeping with a harm-reduction approach to substance use, be on the lookout for the following behaviours or effects:

- increasing tolerance (i.e., needing to take increasingly higher doses to achieve the desired effect)

- withdrawal symptoms (nausea, irritability, nervousness, shaking, or trouble concentrating)

- taking larger-than-recommended doses of prescription medications

- having a persistent desire to reduce drug use and being unsuccessful in your attempts

- spending a lot of time obtaining drugs, using drugs, or recovering from using drugs

- giving up or reducing participation in social, academic, occupational, or recreational activities

- drug-related legal problems

- spending a significant amount of money to acquire drugs

- feeling shame or embarrassment because of the stigma associated with substance use.

Binge Drinking

Many television shows or movies about university include partying and drinking scenes. What they don't mention is that binge drinking can be a symptom of an alcohol use disorder. The Centre for Addiction and Mental Health defines binge drinking as consuming five or more units of alcohol (one unit is equal to one five-ounce glass of wine, one cocktail or highball, or one regular-sized can or bottle of regular-strength beer) in a single sitting. Continuous bouts of binge drinking can cause irreparable damage to your brain, liver, and digestive system. Students who engage in binge drinking tend to have lower grades and are more likely to drop out of school than their peers who do not binge drink. Binge drinking also puts you at greater risk for alcohol-related events, such as violence or traffic accidents. Those who choose to binge drink are also at greater risk for developing serious mental illnesses such as depression and suicidal thoughts.

FYI ---------- *Practising Responsible Drinking* ----------

If you choose to drink, try to keep your weekly alcohol consumption under ten to fifteen drinks, depending on your size. The daily limit for men is considered three drinks per day, whereas most women are advised to consume no more than two drinks per day. One way for you to reduce your consumption is to simply buy less – you'll consume less. Buying alcohol in bulk may be cheaper, but you could end up drinking more simply because it's there. Another thing you can do is drink more slowly and resist pressure to pick up the pace.

Most important, avoid drinking when you're taking medicine or other drugs, dealing with health problems, making important decisions, or providing others with care.

Cannabis Use

Cannabis use has increased among students over the last ten years, especially since it became legal in 2019. Many students use cannabis recreationally without issue, but frequent use has been linked to the abuse of other drugs, including alcohol, and a 2015 study by Diana Keith and colleagues published in the *American Journal on Addictions* shows that it can increase the risk of depression in undergraduate students. To avoid overconsumption, limit the amount you purchase at any given time, and use a smaller amount less often.

Prescription Drugs

Misuse of prescription drugs is a growing issue. Substances of particular concern include opioids (e.g., Vicodin, oxycodone, Dilaudid), prescription sedatives (e.g., Xanax, Valium), and stimulants (e.g., Adderall, Ritalin, Concerta). A 2018 Canadian Centre on Substance Use and Addiction study found that between 4 and 6 percent of Canadian postsecondary students reported using prescription drugs for an unintended purpose, the most common being to enhance their academic performance. Research suggests, however, that those who use these drugs recreationally have lower grades compared to those who do not.

And contrary to common belief, taking prescription drugs is not less risky than taking illegal street drugs. You might forget how many pills you've taken in one sitting and use more, increasing the risk of overdose. Or you might inadvertently mix them with alcohol or another substance, which can lead to pronounced impairment.

Prescription drugs may be manufactured by pharmaceutical companies, but using them for an unintended use can have major, unintended physical side effects. For example, Adderall XR has been shown to cause rare, spontaneous, and fatal cardiovascular events among adult populations. Reports of cardiovascular side effects, mental health disorders such as psychosis and depression, and death have led warnings to be issued for other methylphenidate-based prescription medications such as Ritalin and Concerta. And pre-existing health conditions can be exacerbated by taking prescription medications. You may think prescription drugs are safe because they're manufactured by pharmaceutical companies, but all prescription drugs have side effects, and it's important to see a doctor before using them to ensure they're safe for you.

Reducing the Harmful Effects of Prescription Drugs

FYI

If you're taking prescription drugs for an unintended purpose, the fewer days in a row you use a drug the better. Here are some harm-reduction methods to consider.

- Set a time limit for when you'll be using and when you'll stop using the drugs, and plan out the amount you'll use in that time.

If you plan to stop using medications at 4 p.m., watch the time, keep track of how much you're using, remind yourself of your plan, and stick to it. Have something to eat or drink when you reach your limit to help you feel satisfied.

- If you think you're overusing, try cutting back your use to every other day. Plan out the days you won't be taking the drug, including how you'll spend your time and energy.

If you're having trouble limiting your drug use, try talking to someone who is caring and understanding.

Illegal Drugs

Illegal drugs are, by definition, not legal and in many places you could face charges for using them or having them in your possession. These drugs include stimulants such as cocaine or MDMA, opioids such as heroin, and psychedelics such as LSD or psilocybin ("magic") mushrooms. Some of these drugs such as MDMA are considered "party drugs," but using them can bring risks to your physical, social, emotional, and academic well-being. Cocaine and heroin, for instance, are incredibly addictive and prolonged use of any of these substances can put you at greater risk for experiencing a substance abuse disorder or mental illnesses such as depression and anxiety. Frequent users might find it difficult to regulate their moods when they're not using.

If you're using any illegal drugs, there are ways you can reduce their overall harm. First, injecting a drug carries more risk than smoking, inhaling, or swallowing it. If you do inject drugs, use new syringes and avoid injections in the neck. Second, don't take these types of drugs alone. They can contain substances such as fentanyl, which can cause overdoses and death.

Suicidal Thoughts

According to research by Allan Schwartz and Mark Loftis and colleagues, suicide is one of the leading causes of death among college students. Although this fact is alarming, it's important to understand that not everyone who thinks about suicide completes suicide. Suicidal thoughts (or suicidal ideation) mean thinking about or planning to complete suicide. These thoughts can range from thoughts in passing to detailed plans. Many people have suicidal thoughts, and they frequently occur when they're experiencing abnormal stress or depression. They don't always mean that someone is going to complete suicide, but they should be taken seriously because these types of thoughts put people at greater risk for attempting suicide.

Some of the symptoms associated with suicidal ideation are as follows:

- feeling or appearing to feel intolerable emotional pain

- feeling or appearing to feel trapped

- having or appearing to have an abnormal preoccupation with dying or death

- being or appearing to be agitated or in a heightened state of anxiety

GETTING HELP
National Substance Use and Addiction Resources
The Canadian Centre on Substance Use and Addiction is a nongovernmental organization that provides advanced solutions to address alcohol- and other drug-related harms. It provides up-to-date information about substance-use issues in Canada and has information about treatment, support, and recovery.

The Centre for Addiction and Mental Health is Canada's largest centre for addictions and mental health services. Its website provides information on addictions and substance-use programming in each province and online. It also contains information on the types of addictions commonly experienced by Canadians and their symptoms.

- experiencing or appearing to experience changes in routines, behaviours, personality, sleeping patterns, or drug and alcohol consumption

- increased isolation.

These symptoms can be difficult to notice because most students who experience suicidal thoughts don't talk about their feelings with others. If you experience these feelings or know someone who is, there are trained professionals ready to help.

If you or someone you know is at risk of harming themselves or others, please contact 911 immediately.

Prevention Helplines

Suicide Prevention Helplines and Online Resources

Throughout Canada, you can call 911 if you or someone you know is at *immediate risk* of causing harm to themselves or others.

Alberta Health Link (811) and Mental Health Helpline (1-877-303-2642)
BC Suicide Helpline 1-800-784-2433 (1-800-SUICIDE)
Manitoba Suicide Prevention and Support Line (1-877-435-7170)
New Brunswick Provincial Suicide Prevention Crisis Line (1-800-667-5005)
Newfoundland Mental Health Crisis Line (1-888-737-4668)
Northwest Territories Provincial Information and Help Line (1-800-661-0844)
Nova Scotia Provincial Online Resources Crisis Line (1-888-429-8167)
Nunavut Kamatsiaqtut Help Line (1-800-265-3333)
Ontario Telehealth (1-866-797-0000)
PEI Suicide Helpline (1-800-218-2885)
Quebec Suicide Prevention Helpline (1-866-277-3553)
Regina Crisis Line (306-525-5333)
Saskatchewan National Crisis Line (1-833-456-566)
Saskatoon Mobile Crisis Line (306-933-6200)
Yukon Distress Support Line (1-800-563-0808)

Online Resources

Each province and territory has a website dedicated to suicide ideation that can be accessed by searching for "suicide" and the name of the province. In addition, consult the websites of the following organizations:

- Alberta Health Services
- BC Crisis Centre
- Canadian Association for Suicide Prevention
- Crisis Services Canada
- Ontario Association for Suicide Prevention
- Reason to Live Manitoba
- Saskatchewan Division, Canadian Mental Health Association
- Yukon Youth (BYTE)

KEEPING A HEALTHY MIND

My time in undergrad wasn't what I expected it would be. I had more trouble making friends and keeping my grades up than I had anticipated. And I didn't expect to experience symptoms of anxiety and depression in my first year. Fortunately, I eventually learned that I had friends that I could talk to and mental health professionals ready to help me through those hard times.

Those people are the reason for my success. After talking to others about my emotional struggles and finding strategies that fit my needs, I got better grades and was accepted into a master's program. In graduate school, I excelled and gained entrance into one of the top PhD programs in the country. The tools I learned back then continue to help me now. I have a good professional life that includes teaching undergraduate courses, publishing research, speaking at conferences, and working one-on-one with students. I have wonderful colleagues who I look forward to seeing every day and consider the university environment my home.

But none of this would have been possible if I had not asked for help or reached out to others. The only reason things got better is that I talked to people about the problems I was experiencing and committed myself to learning different strategies for coping with these challenges. However, as became clear when I started working on this book and experienced a wave of self-doubt, I still struggle with mental health challenges today. But I now know that I have the resources and skills to manage them and the experience to recognize when I need extra help.

It's my greatest hope that in reading this book, you've found strategies and information that will help you succeed in university and maintain and remain in good mental health. There are three take-away messages I'd like to leave you with:

Have compassion for yourself and for others.
As you've learned throughout this book, navigating college or university can be fun and invigorating but there will be setbacks. Having compassion for your trials and tribulations means taking time to step back and think about what you're dealing with and how you would think about someone else who is experiencing the same thing. Would you disparage them in the same way you disparage yourself? Would you think less of them? Would you think they're unworthy of help?

Talk about it.
You're not an island. Talk to your friends and family members about things that are bothering you. Maybe one of them has already found a solution to a particular problem and can give you advice on how to overcome it. Maybe they haven't figured it out yet, and you can both work through it together. Perhaps family members can give you extra emotional, financial, or social support in your time of need. By talking to others, you're opening yourself up to more solutions.

Talking with others will make that road easier to travel for yourself and others in the future. There's still a lot of stigma attached to getting help. You have the power to change those narratives by helping to bring mental health conversations into the light.

When you do find others to talk to, make sure they're the people who can best support you. You might run into people who'll say "It's just a phase," "You'll get over it," or "Other people have way worse problems." While some of these statements might be true, they aren't especially helpful for addressing your needs. Don't be afraid to turn to someone else for help if your first confidante is dismissive. Find people who can listen effectively to your challenges and help you find positive solutions.

Ask for help and don't get swamped.
All successful students need help from someone at some point. Unfortunately, students commonly wait until they're swamped by social, academic, or emotional problems before talking to others. Some of the busiest times in campus service centres are at the end of the semester, because students let their problems build up until they hit a breaking point in December or April. You don't need to be among them. With the tools you've learned in this book, you can avoid this pitfall by checking in with yourself, practising self-care strategies in all aspects of your life, and getting help sooner rather than later.

The fact that you picked up and read this book means you're on the right path. By taking care of yourself you're lighting the way for others.

ACKNOWLEDGMENTS

This book would not have been possible without the guidance and support of my editors at UBC Press. I'm extremely grateful to Melissa Pitts and Kerry Kilmartin for giving me the opportunity to write this book and to Lesley Erickson, Ann Macklem, and Nadine Pedersen for their tireless editing and exceptionally thoughtful feedback. I had no idea what I was getting into, but you all made this one of the most enjoyable and rewarding experiences of my academic career. Thank you!

In addition to the staff at UBC Press, I am exceptionally grateful to professors Neil Guppy, Rima Wilkes, and Kerry Greer. Neil read every chapter, answered my onslaught of questions, and eased my fears about the publishing process. Rima continuously challenged me to push the envelope in my work and develop my own voice. And Kerry's suggestions helped me keep the aim of the project in mind and to see this path more clearly. Combined, you all kept me feeling motivated to finish this work to the best of my ability.

All my students, current and past, informed some aspect of this book. I am so thankful to have had the opportunity to learn from all of you. Special thanks to Colleen Chambers, Emily Chan, Cecilia Federizon, and Julian Lao, who graciously provided me with their own stories of undergraduate challenges. I also want to thank Andy Holmes, who not only contributed a personal story for the book, but also provided thoughtful feedback on chapter content. You all are such amazing, smart, and caring people and I am exceptionally appreciative for your willingness to help.

The anonymous reviewers of this book deserve special thanks. I would also like to acknowledge the special contributions of Annette Angell and the staff of the AMS Sexual Assault Support Centre at UBC; Kate Jaffe and researchers at the BC Centre on Substance Use; Rachelle Malette and staff at the Three Oaks shelter; registered nurse Agata Leibrock at St. Joseph's Healthcare Hamilton, Youth Wellness Centre; and Hélène Frohard-Dourlent at the UBC Equity and Inclusion Office. Your time, energy, and feedback meant the world to me and were so greatly appreciated.

Last, but not least, I have to thank my friends and family. Most of all, Kris Clark. When I told you I had been offered the opportunity to write a book you said, "Of course!" You never doubted me, especially when I doubted myself. You also maintained that same level of unwavering enthusiasm and support for the two years it took me to finish writing this work. This came at an expense to yourself and your free time. Not many people have your compassion, and I'm so thankful you share it with me.

I would also like to recognize the contributions of my parents (Diane Malette-Brownson and Chris Malette) to this work. You read chapters, gave feedback, and made fun of my spelling. You pushed me to do better and to be better. My want to help others comes from both of you and is at the core of this work. I love you. Thank you.

SOURCES

Introduction: Knowing You're Not Alone

Abbey, S., Charbonneau, M., Tranulis, C., Moss, P., Baici, W., Dabby, L., ... & Paré, M. (2011). Stigma and discrimination. *Canadian Journal of Psychiatry, 56*(10), 1–9.

Abolghasemi, A., & Varaniyab, S.T. (2010). Resilience and perceived stress: Predictors of life satisfaction in the students of success and failure. *Procedia–Social and Behavioral Sciences, 5,* 748–52.

American College Health Association. (2016). Ontario Canada Reference Group: Executive summary. http://oucha.ca/pdf/2016_NCHA-II_WEB_SPRING_2016_ONTARIO_CANADA_ REFERENCE_GROUP_EXECUTIVE_SUMMARY.pdf.

American Medical Association. (1999). Health literacy: Report of the Council on Scientific Affairs. *JAMA, 281*(6), 552–57.

American Psychiatric Association. (2013). *Diagnostic and statistical manual of mental disorders.* Arlington: American Psychiatric Publishing.

Bourget, B., & Chenier, R. (2007). *Mental health literacy in Canada: Phase one report mental health literacy project.* Ottawa: Canadian Alliance on Mental Illness and Mental Health.

Corrigan, P.W., Lurie, B.D., Goldman, H.H., Slopen, N., Medasani, K., & Phelan, S. (2005). How adolescents perceive the stigma of mental illness and alcohol abuse. *Psychiatric Services, 56*(5), 544–50.

Corrigan, P.W., & Miller, F.E. (2004). Shame, blame, and contamination: A review of the impact of mental illness stigma on family members. *Journal of Mental Health, 13*(6), 537–48.

Corrigan, P.W., & Watson, A.C. (2007). The stigma of psychiatric disorders and the gender, ethnicity, and education of the perceiver. *Community Mental Health Journal, 43*(5), 439–58.

Corrigan, P.W., Watson, A.C., Byrne, P., & Davis, K.E. (2005). Mental illness stigma: Problem of public health or social injustice? *Social Work, 50*(4), 363–68.

Eisenberg, D., Downs, M.F., Golberstein, E., & Zivin, K. (2009). Stigma and help seeking for mental health among college students. *Medical Care Research and Review, 66*(5), 522–41.

Eisenberg, D., Gollust, S.E., Golberstein, E., & Hefner, J.L. (2007). Prevalence and correlates of depression, anxiety, and suicidality among university students. *American Journal of Orthopsychiatry, 77*(4), 534–42.

Eisenberg, D., Hunt, J., Speer, N., & Zivin, K. (2011). Mental health service utilization among college students in the United States. *Journal of Nervous and Mental Disease, 199*(5), 301–8.

Hunt, J., & Eisenberg, D. (2010). Mental health problems and help-seeking behavior among college students. *Journal of Adolescent Health, 46*(1), 3–10.

Karpinski, R.I., Kolb, A.M.K., Tetreault, N.A., & Borowski, T.B. (2018). High intelligence: A risk factor for psychological and physiological overexcitabilities. *Intelligence, 66*, 8–23.

Kessler, R.C., Amminger, G.P., Aguilar-Gaxiola, S., Alonso, J., Lee, S., & Üstün, T.B. (2007). Age of onset of mental disorders: A review of recent literature. *Current Opinion in Psychiatry, 20*(4), 359–64.

Mental Health Commission of Canada (2017). Mental health continuum model. https://theworkingmind.ca/sites/default/files/resources/r2mr_poster_en.pdf.

Sandhu, H.S., Arora, A., Brasch, J., & Streiner, D.L. (2019). Mental health stigma: Explicit and implicit attitudes of Canadian undergraduate students, medical school students, and psychiatrists. *Canadian Journal of Psychiatry, 64*(3), 209–17.

World Health Organization. Department of Mental Health, Substance Abuse, Mental Health Evidence and Research Team. (2005). *Mental health atlas 2005.* Geneva: World Health Organization.

Chapter 1: Making the Transition to University

American College Health Association. (2016). Ontario Canada Reference Group: Executive summary. http://oucha.ca/pdf/2016_NCHA-II_WEB_SPRING_2016_ONTARIO_CANADA_REFERENCE_GROUP_EXECUTIVE_SUMMARY.pdf.

Eisenberg, D., Gollust, S.E., Golberstein, E., & Hefner, J.L. (2007). Prevalence and correlates of depression, anxiety, and suicidality among university students. *American Journal of Orthopsychiatry, 77*(4), 534–42.

Rayle, A.D., & Chung, K.Y. (2007). Revisiting first-year college students' mattering: Social support, academic stress, and the mattering experience. *Journal of College Student Retention: Research, Theory and Practice, 9*(1), 21–37.

World Health Organization. (2008). *The global burden of disease: 2004 update.* Geneva: World Health Organization.

Chapter 2: Valuing and Supporting Diversity

Canada Millennium Scholarship Foundation. (2005). *Changing course: Improving Aboriginal access to post-secondary education in Canada.* Millennium Research Note 2. Montreal: Canada Millennium Scholarship Foundation.

SOURCES

Clark, H., Babu, A.S., Wiewel, E.W., Opoku, J., & Crepaz, N. (2017). Diagnosed HIV infection in transgender adults and adolescents: Results from the National HIV Surveillance System, 2009–2014. *AIDS and Behavior, 21*(9), 2774–83.

Fausto-Sterling, A. (1993). The five sexes: Why male and female are not enough. *The Sciences, 33,* 20–25.

Fausto-Sterling, A. (2000). The five sexes, revisited. *The Sciences, 40*(4), 18–23.

Fraga, E.D., Atkinson, D.R., & Wampold, B.E. (2004). Ethnic group preferences for multicultural counseling competencies. *Cultural Diversity and Ethnic Minority Psychology, 10*(1), 53–65.

Hogarth, K. (2015). Home without security and security without home. *Journal of International Migration and Integration, 16*(3), 783–98.

Holmes, D. (2006). Redressing the balance: Canadian university programs in support of Aboriginal students. Ottawa: Association of Universities and Colleges of Canada.

Hudson, N. (2009). Contextualizing outcomes of public schooling: Disparate post-secondary aspirations among Aboriginal and non-Aboriginal secondary students (unpublished master's thesis). University of Toronto. https://tspace.library.utoronto.ca/bitstream/1807/18119/5/hudson_natasha_200911_MA_thesis.pdf.

Kung, W.W. (2004). Cultural and practical barriers to seeking mental health treatment for Chinese Americans. *Journal of Community Psychology, 32*(1), 27–43.

Lambert, M., Zeman, K., Allen, M., & Bussière, P. (2004). Who pursues postsecondary education, who leaves and why: Results from the Youth in Transition Survey. Research paper, Culture, Tourism, and Centre for Education Statistics. https://www150.statcan.gc.ca/n1/en/pub/81-595-m/81-595-m2004026-eng.pdf?st=037_IgzT.

Lee, S., Juon, H.S., Martinez, G., Hsu, C.E., Robinson, E.S., Bawa, J., & Ma, G.X. (2009). Model minority at risk: Expressed needs of mental health by Asian American young adults. *Journal of Community Health, 34*(2), 144–52.

Lehmann, W. (2007). "I just didn't feel like I fit in": The role of habitus in university dropout decisions. *Canadian Journal of Higher Education, 37*(2), 89–110.

Lehmann, W. (2014). Habitus transformation and hidden injuries: Successful working-class university students. *Sociology of Education, 87*(1), 1–15.

Lehmann, W. (2019). Forms of capital in working-class students' transition from university to employment. *Journal of Education and Work, 32*(4), 347–59.

Locks, A.M., Hurtado, S., Bowman, N.A., & Oseguera, L. (2008). Extending notions of campus climate and diversity to students' transition to college. *Review of Higher Education, 31*(3), 257–85.

Malatest, R.A. (2004). *Aboriginal peoples and post-secondary education: What educators have learned.* Montreal: Canada Millennium Scholarship Foundation.

Malette, N., & Guppy, N. (2016). Educational attainment among Canadians: Open and competitive or closed and sponsored? In E. Grabb, M. Hwang, & J. Reitz (Eds.), *Social Inequality in Canada* (104–12). Toronto: Oxford University Press.

Massey, D.S., & Owens, J. (2014). Mediators of stereotype threat among black college students. *Ethnic and Racial Studies, 37*(3), 557–75.

Olson, J., Schrager, S.M., Belzer, M., Simons, L.K., & Clark, L.F. (2015). Baseline physiologic and psychosocial characteristics of transgender youth seeking care for gender dysphoria. *Journal of Adolescent Health, 57*(4), 374–80.

Pieterse, A.L., Carter, R.T., Evans, S.A., & Walter, R.A. (2010). An exploratory examination of the associations among racial and ethnic discrimination, racial climate, and trauma-related symptoms in a college student population. *Journal of Counselling Psychology, 57*(3), 255–63.

Pike, G.R., & Kuh, G.D. (2005). First- and second-generation college students: A comparison of their engagement and intellectual development. *Journal of Higher Education, 76*(3), 276–300.

Reisner, S.L., Poteat, T., Keatley, J., Cabral, M., Mothopeng, T., Dunham, E., ... & Baral, S.D. (2016). Global health burden and needs of transgender populations: A review. *The Lancet, 388*(10042), 412–36.

Smedley, B.D., Myers, H.F., & Harrell, S.P. (1993). Minority-status stresses and the college adjustment of ethnic minority freshmen. *Journal of Higher Education, 64*(4), 434–52.

Solorzano, D., Ceja, M., & Yosso, T. (2000). Critical race theory, racial microaggressions, and campus racial climate: The experiences of African American college students. *Journal of Negro Education, 69*(1–2), 60–73.

St. Denis, V., & Hampton, E. (2002). Literature review on racism and the effects on Aboriginal education. Report prepared for Minister's National Working Group on Education. Ottawa: Indian and Northern Affairs Canada.

Stebleton, M.J., Soria, K.M., & Huesman Jr., R.L. (2014). First-generation students' sense of belonging, mental health, and use of counseling services at public research universities. *Journal of College Counseling, 17*(1), 6–20.

Stephens, N.M., Fryberg, S.A., Markus, H.R., Johnson, C.S., & Covarrubias, R. (2012). Unseen disadvantage: How American universities' focus on independence undermines the academic performance of first-generation college students. *Journal of Personality and Social Psychology, 102*(6), 1178–97.

Suzuki, B.H. (2002). Revisiting the model minority stereotype: Implications for student affairs practice and higher education. *New Directions for Student Services, 97,* 21–32.

Truth and Reconciliation Commission of Canada. (2015). *Truth and Reconciliation Commission of Canada: Calls to action.* Truth and Reconciliation Commission of Canada.

Walpole, M. (2003). Socioeconomic status and college: How SES affects college experiences and outcomes. *Review of Higher Education, 27*(1), 45–73.

Zivin, K., Eisenberg, D., Gollust, S.E., & Golberstein, E. (2009). Persistence of mental health problems and needs in a college student population. *Journal of Affective Disorders, 117*(3), 180–85.

Chapter 3: Understanding Mental Health

Abbey, S., Charbonneau, M., Tranulis, C., Moss, P., Baici, W., Dabby, L., ... & Paré, M. (2011). Stigma and discrimination. *Canadian Journal of Psychiatry, 56*(10), 1–9.

Abolghasemi, A., & Varaniyab, S.T. (2010). Resilience and perceived stress: Predictors of life satisfaction in the students of success and failure. *Procedia–Social and Behavioral Sciences, 5*, 748–52.

Cheng, S.T., Tsui, P.K., & Lam, J.H. (2015). Improving mental health in health care practitioners: Randomized controlled trial of a gratitude intervention. *Journal of Consulting and Clinical Psychology, 83*(1), 177.

Fawcett, S., Abeykoon, P., Arora, M., Dobe, M., Galloway-Gilliam, L., Liburd, L., & Munodawafa, D. (2010). Constructing an action agenda for community empowerment at the 7th Global Conference on Health Promotion in Nairobi. *Global Health Promotion, 17*(4), 52–56.

Han, M., & Pong, H. (2015). Mental health help-seeking behaviors among Asian American community college students: The effect of stigma, cultural barriers, and acculturation. *Journal of College Student Development, 56*(1), 1–14.

Hunt, J., & Eisenberg, D. (2010). Mental health problems and help-seeking behavior among college students. *Journal of Adolescent Health, 46*(1), 3–10.

Jorm, A.F., Korten, A.E., Jacomb, P.A., Christensen, H., Rodgers, B., & Pollitt, P. (1997). "Mental health literacy": A survey of the public's ability to recognise mental disorders and their beliefs about the effectiveness of treatment. *Medical Journal of Australia, 166*(4), 182–86.

Kessler, R.C., Amminger, G.P., Aguilar-Gaxiola, S., Alonso, J., Lee, S., & Üstün, T.B. (2007). Age of onset of mental disorders: A review of recent literature. *Current Opinion in Psychiatry, 20*(4), 359–64.

Kotov, R., Gamez, W., Schmidt, F., & Watson, D. (2010). Linking "big" personality traits to anxiety, depressive, and substance use disorders: A meta-analysis. *Psychological Bulletin, 136*(5), 768–821.

Kutcher, S., Wei, Y., & Coniglio, C. (2016). Mental health literacy: Past, present, and future. *Canadian Journal of Psychiatry, 61*(3), 154–58.

Mayne, D.J., Morgan, G.G., Jalaludin, B.B., & Bauman, A.E. (2018). Does walkability contribute to geographic variation in psychosocial distress? A spatial analysis of 91,142 members of the 45 and Up Study in Sydney, Australia. *International Journal of Environmental Research and Public Health, 15*(2), 275.

Mental Health Commission of Canada (2017). Mental Health Continuum Model. https://theworkingmind.ca/sites/default/files/resources/r2mr_poster_en.pdf.

Chapter 4: Meeting Academic Hurdles Head-On

Cepeda, N.J., Pashler, H., Vul, E., Wixted, J.T., & Rohrer, D. (2006). Distributed practice in verbal recall tasks: A review and quantitative synthesis. *Psychological Bulletin, 132*(3), 354–80.

Hoffman, E.M. (2014). Faculty and student relationships: Context matters. *College Teaching, 62*(1), 13–19.

Leu, K. (2017). Beginning college students who change their majors within 3 years of enrollment. Data Point, NCES 2018–434. National Center for Education Statistics.

O'Keeffe, P. (2013). A sense of belonging: Improving student retention. *College Student Journal, 47*(4), 605–13.

Parkman, A. (2016). The imposter phenomenon in higher education: Incidence and impact. *Journal of Higher Education Theory and Practice, 16*(1), 51–60.

Strayhorn, T.L. (2012). *College students' sense of belonging: A key to educational success for all students.* London: Routledge.

Chapter 5: Making Time for Friends and Extracurriculars

Armstrong, E.A., & Hamilton, L.T. (2013). *Paying for the party.* Cambridge: Harvard University Press.

Kadison, R., & DiGeronimo, T.F. (2004). *College of the overwhelmed: The campus mental health crisis and what to do about it.* San Francisco: Jossey-Bass.

O'Keeffe, P. (2013). A sense of belonging: Improving student retention. *College Student Journal, 47*(4), 605–13.

Parkman, A. (2016). The imposter phenomenon in higher education: Incidence and impact. *Journal of Higher Education Theory and Practice, 16*(1), 51–60.

Strayhorn, T.L. (2012). *College students' sense of belonging: A key to educational success for all students.* London: Routledge.

Chapter 6: Going Out and Staying In

Armstrong, E.A., & Hamilton, L.T. (2013). *Paying for the party.* Cambridge: Harvard University Press.

Cassidy, C., Steenbeek, A., Langille, D., Martin-Misener, R., & Curran, J. (2017). Development of a behavior change intervention to improve sexual health service use among university undergraduate students: Mixed methods study protocol. *JMIR Research Protocols, 6*(11), e217.

Cragg, A., Steenbeek, A., Asbridge, M., Andreou, P., & Langille, D. (2016). Sexually transmitted infection testing among heterosexual Maritime Canadian university students engaging in different levels of sexual risk taking. *Canadian Journal of Public Health, 107*(2), 149–54.

Fisher, B. (2000). *The sexual victimization of college women.* Washington, DC: US Department of Justice, Office of Justice Programs, National Institute of Justice.

Johnson, L.M., Matthews, T.L., & Napper, S.L. (2016). Sexual orientation and sexual assault victimization among US college students. *Social Science Journal, 53*(2), 174–83.

Kadison, R., & DiGeronimo, T.F. (2004). *College of the overwhelmed: The campus mental health crisis and what to do about it.* San Francisco: Jossey-Bass.

Kenney, S.R., Ott, M., Meisel, M.K., & Barnett, N.P. (2017). Alcohol perceptions and behavior in a residential peer social network. *Addictive Behaviors, 64,* 143–47.

Lindo, J.M., Siminski, P., & Swensen, I.D. (2018). College party culture and sexual assault. *American Economic Journal: Applied Economics, 10*(1), 236–65.

Locks, A.M., Hurtado, S., Bowman, N.A., & Oseguera, L. (2008). Extending notions of campus climate and diversity to students' transition to college. *Review of Higher Education, 31*(3), 257–85.

Long, S.M., Ullman, S.E., Long, L.M., Mason, G.E., & Starzynski, L.L. (2007). Women's experiences of male-perpetrated sexual assault by sexual orientation. *Violence and Victims, 22*(6), 684–701.

Chapter 7: Doing It All and Still Having Time for You

Balchin, R., Linde, J., Blackhurst, D., Rauch, H.., & Schönbächler, G. (2016). Sweating away depression? The impact of intensive exercise on depression. *Journal of Affective Disorders, 200,* 218–21.

Barton, J., & Pretty, J. (2010). What is the best dose of nature and green exercise for improving mental health? A multi-study analysis. *Environmental Science and Technology, 44*(10), 3947–55.

Bratman, G.N., Hamilton, J.P., & Daily, G.C. (2012). The impacts of nature experience on human cognitive function and mental health. *Annals of the New York Academy of Sciences, 1249*(1), 118–36.

Chen, H.M., Tsai, C.M., Wu, Y.C., Lin, K.C., & Lin, C.C. (2015). Randomised controlled trial on the effectiveness of home-based walking exercise on anxiety, depression and cancer-related symptoms in patients with lung cancer. *British Journal of Cancer, 112*(3), 438–45.

Cheng, S.T., Tsui, P.K., & Lam, J.H. (2015). Improving mental health in health care practitioners: Randomized controlled trial of a gratitude intervention. *Journal of Consulting and Clinical Psychology, 83*(1), 177.

De Moor, M., & De Geus, E. (2018). Causality in the associations between exercise, personality, and mental health. In H. Budde & M. Wegner (Eds.), *The exercise effect on mental health: Neurobiological mechanisms* (67–99). Milton Park: Taylor and Francis.

Deslandes, A., Moraes, H., Ferreira, C., Veiga, H., Silveira, H., Mouta, R., ... & Laks, J. (2009). Exercise and mental health: Many reasons to move. *Neuropsychobiology, 59*(4), 191–98.

SOURCES

Figueiro, M.G., Wood, B., Plitnick, B., & Rea, M.S. (2011). The impact of light from computer monitors on the melatonin levels in college students. *Biog Amines, 25,* 106–16.

Gómez-Pinilla, F. (2008). Brain foods: The effects of nutrients on brain function. *Nature Reviews Neuroscience, 9*(7), 568–78.

Imayama, I., Alfano, C.M., Bertram, L.A.C., Wang, C., Xiao, L., Duggan, C., ... & McTiernan, A. (2011). Effects of 12-month exercise on health-related quality of life: A randomized controlled trial. *Preventive Medicine, 52*(5), 344–51.

Jacka, F.N., Kremer, P.J., Berk, M., de Silva-Sanigorski, A.M., Moodie, M., Leslie, E.R., ... & Swinburn, B.A. (2011). A prospective study of diet quality and mental health in adolescents. *PloS ONE, 6*(9), e24805.

Kavussanu, M., & Roberts, G.C. (1998). Motivation in physical activity contexts: The relationship of perceived motivational climate to intrinsic motivation and self-efficacy. *Journal of Sport and Exercise Psychology, 20*(3), 264–80.

Knapen, J., Vancampfort, D., Moriën, Y., & Marchal, Y. (2015). Exercise therapy improves both mental and physical health in patients with major depression. *Disability and Rehabilitation, 37*(16), 1490–95.

Manber, R., & Carney, C.E. (2015). *Treatment plans and interventions for insomnia: A case formulation approach.* New York: Guilford.

Middelkamp, J., van Rooijen, M., Wolfhagen, P., & Steenbergen, B. (2017). The effects of a self-efficacy intervention on exercise behavior of fitness club members in 52 weeks and long-term relationships of transtheoretical model constructs. *Journal of Sports Science and Medicine, 16*(2), 163–71.

Mikkelsen, K., Stojanovska, L., Polenakovic, M., Bosevski, M., & Apostolopoulos, V. (2017). Exercise and mental health. *Maturitas, 106,* 48–56.

Newman, A.B., Nieto, F.J., Guidry, U., Lind, B.K., Redline, S., Shahar, E., ... & Quan, S.F. (2001). Relation of sleep-disordered breathing to cardiovascular disease risk factors: The Sleep Heart Health Study. *American Journal of Epidemiology, 154*(1), 50–59.

Passmore, A., & French, D. (2000). A model of leisure and mental health in Australian adolescents. *Behaviour Change, 17*(3), 208–20.

Penedo, F.J., & Dahn, J.R. (2005). Exercise and well-being: A review of mental and physical health benefits associated with physical activity. *Current Opinion in Psychiatry, 18*(2), 189–93.

Ponde, M.P., & Santana, V.S. (2000). Participation in leisure activities: Is it a protective factor for women's mental health? *Journal of Leisure Research, 32*(4), 457–72.

Potter, G.D., Skene, D.J., Arendt, J., Cade, J.E., Grant, P.J., & Hardie, L.J. (2016). Circadian rhythm and sleep disruption: Causes, metabolic consequences, and countermeasures. *Endocrine Reviews, 37*(6), 584–608.

Roehrs, T., & Roth, T. (2001). Sleep, sleepiness, and alcohol use. *Alcohol Research and Health, 25*(2), 101–9.

Sabiston, C.M., O'Loughlin, E., Brunet, J., Chaiton, M., Low, N.C., Barnett, T., & O'Loughlin, J. (2013). Linking depression symptom trajectories in adolescence to physical activity and team sports participation in young adults. *Preventive Medicine*, 56(2), 95–98.

Scarapicchia, T.M.F., Amireault, S., Faulkner, G., & Sabiston, C.M. (2017). Social support and physical activity participation among healthy adults: A systematic review of prospective studies. *International Review of Sport and Exercise Psychology*, 10(1), 50–83.

Simpson, N.S., Gibbs, E.L., & Matheson, G.O. (2017). Optimizing sleep to maximize performance: Implications and recommendations for elite athletes. *Scandinavian Journal of Medicine and Science in Sports*, 27(3), 266–74.

Snel, J., & Lorist, M.M. (2011). Effects of caffeine on sleep and cognition. *Progress in Brain Research*, 190, 105–17.

Soysa, C.K., & Wilcomb, C.J. (2015). Mindfulness, self-compassion, self-efficacy, and gender as predictors of depression, anxiety, stress, and well-being. *Mindfulness*, 6(2), 217–26.

Thorén, P., Floras, J.S., Hoffmann, P., & Seals, D.R. (1990). Endorphins and exercise: Physiological mechanisms and clinical implications. *Medicine and Science in Sports and Exercise*, 22(4), 417–28.

Walsh, R. (2011). Lifestyle and mental health. *American Psychologist*, 66(7), 579–92.

Williamson, A.M., & Feyer, A.M. (2000). Moderate sleep deprivation produces impairments in cognitive and motor performance equivalent to legally prescribed levels of alcohol intoxication. *Occupational and Environmental Medicine*, 57(10), 649–55.

Chapter 8: Recognizing the Signs of Mental Illness

American College Health Association. (2016). Ontario Canada Reference Group: Executive summary. http://oucha.ca/pdf/2016_NCHA-II_WEB_SPRING_2016_ONTARIO_CANADA_REFERENCE_GROUP_EXECUTIVE_SUMMARY.pdf.

American Psychiatric Association. (2013). *Diagnostic and statistical manual of mental disorders*. Philadelphia: American Psychiatric Association.

Archie, S., Kazemi, A.Z., & Akhtar-Danesh, N. (2012). Concurrent binge drinking and depression among Canadian youth: Prevalence, patterns, and suicidality. *Alcohol*, 46(2), 165–72.

Canadian Centre on Substance Use and Addiction. (2018). Non-medical prescription stimulant use among post-secondary students. https://www.ccsa.ca/sites/default/files/2019–04/CCSA-Non-Medical-Prescription-Stimulant-Use-Students-Summary-2018-en.pdf.

Canadian Centre on Substance Use and Addiction. (2019). Alcohol policy framework. http://www.camh.ca/alcoholpolicy.

Centre for Addiction and Mental Health (Canada). (2019). Partying and getting drunk. https://www.camh.ca/en/health-info/guides-and-publications/partying-and-getting-drunk.

Chiauzzi, E., DasMahapatra, P., & Black, R.A. (2013). Risk behaviours and drug use: A latent class analysis of heavy episodic drinking in first-year college students. *Psychology of Addictive Behaviors, 27*(4), 974.

DeSantis, A.D., & Hane, A.C. (2010). "Adderall is definitely not a drug": Justifications for the illegal use of ADHD stimulants. *Substance Use and Misuse, 45*(1–2), 31–46.

Eisenberg, D., Golberstein, E., & Gollust, S.E. (2007). Help-seeking and access to mental health care in a university student population. *Medical Care, 47*(7), 594–601.

Eisenberg, D., Gollust, S.E., Golberstein, E., & Hefner, J.L. (2007). Prevalence and correlates of depression, anxiety, and suicidality among university students. *American Journal of Orthopsychiatry, 77*(4), 534–42.

Garlow, S.J., Rosenberg, J., Moore, J.D., Haas, A.P., Koestner, B., Hendin, H., & Nemeroff, C.B. (2008). Depression, desperation, and suicidal ideation in college students: Results from the American Foundation for Suicide Prevention College Screening Project at Emory University. *Depression and Anxiety, 25*(6), 482–88.

Jennison, K.M. (2004). The short-term effects and unintended long-term consequences of binge drinking in college: A 10-year follow-up study. *American Journal of Drug and Alcohol Abuse, 30*(3), 659–84.

Kadison, R., & DiGeronimo, T.F. (2004). *College of the overwhelmed: The campus mental health crisis and what to do about it.* San Francisco: Jossey-Bass.

Keith, D.R., Hart, C.L., McNeil, M.P., Silver, R., & Goodwin, R.D. (2015). Frequent marijuana use, binge drinking and mental health problems among undergraduates. *American Journal on Addictions, 24*(6), 499–506.

Keski-Rahkonen, A., & Mustelin, L. (2016). Epidemiology of eating disorders in Europe: Prevalence, incidence, comorbidity, course, consequences, and risk factors. *Current Opinion in Psychiatry, 29*(6), 340–45.

Loftis, M.A., Michael, T., & Luke, C. (2019). College student suicide risk: The relationship between alexithymia, impulsivity, and internal locus of control. *International Journal of Educational Psychology, 8*(3), 246–69.

Low, K.G., & Gendaszek, A.E. (2002). Illicit use of psychostimulants among college students: A preliminary study. *Psychology, Health and Medicine, 7*(3), 283–87.

Okoro, C.A., Brewer, R.D., Naimi, T.S., Moriarty, D.G., Giles, W.H., & Mokdad, A.H. (2004). Binge drinking and health-related quality of life: Do popular perceptions match reality? *American Journal of Preventive Medicine, 26*(3), 230–33.

O'Malley, P.M., & Johnston, L.D. (2002). Epidemiology of alcohol and other drug use among American college students. *Journal of Studies on Alcohol*, supplement, (14), 23–39.

Ploskonka, R.A., & Servaty-Seib, H.L. (2015). Belongingness and suicidal ideation in college students. *Journal of American College Health, 63*(2), 81–87.

Preston, K.L., Kowalczyk, W.J., Phillips, K.A., Jobes, M.L., Vahabzadeh, M., Lin, J.L., ... & Epstein, D.H. (2018). Before and after: Craving, mood, and background stress in the hours surrounding drug use and stressful events in patients with opioid-use disorder. *Psychopharmacology, 235*(9), 2713–23.

Schaffer, M., Jeglic, E.L., & Stanley, B. (2008). The relationship between suicidal behavior, ideation, and binge drinking among college students. *Archives of Suicide Research, 12*(2), 124–32.

Schwartz, A.J. (2006). College student suicide in the United States: 1990–1991 through 2003–2004. *Journal of American College Health, 54*(6), 341–52.

Shinew, K.J., & Parry, D.C. (2005). Examining college students' participation in the leisure pursuits of drinking and illegal drug use. *Journal of Leisure Research, 37*(3), 364–86.

Subramaniam, G.A., Liu, D., & Larimer, M.E. (2017). Perceived academic benefit is associated with nonmedical prescription stimulant use among college students. *Addiction Behavior, 76*, 27–33.

Wechsler, H., Dowdall, G.W., Davenport, A., & Castillo, S. (1995). Correlates of college student binge drinking. *American Journal of Public Health, 85*(7), 921–26.

Zivin, K., Eisenberg, D., Gollust, S.E., & Golberstein, E. (2009). Persistence of mental health problems and needs in a college student population. *Journal of Affective Disorders, 117*(3), 180–85.

INDEX

INDEX

NICOLE MALETTE is an instructor and PhD candidate in the Department of Sociology at the University of British Columbia. Her research focuses on how post-secondary institutional contexts impact undergraduate student mental health and mental health service-use.